A FRIENDLY GUIDE TO JOHN'S GOSPEL

Mary Coloe

Published in Australia by Garratt Publishing 32 Glenvale Crescent Mulgrave, Vic. 3170

www.garrattpublishing.com.au

Copyright © Mary Coloe 2013

All rights reserved. Except as provided by the Australian copyright law, no part of this book may be reproduced in any way without permission in writing from the publisher.

Design and typesetting by Greg Nelson
Cover Design by Lynne Muir
Text editing by Geraldine Corridon
Images: Mary Coloe & Thinkstock.com

Scripture quotations are drawn from the New Revised Standard Version of the Bible, copyright © 1989 by the Division of Christian Education of the National Council of the Churches of Christ in the USA. Used by permission. All rights reserved.

Nihil Obstat: Reverend Gerard Diamond MA (Oxon), LSS, D.Theol - Diocesan Censor
Imprimatur: Monsignor Greg Bennet - Vicar General
Date: 4 August 2012

The Nihil Obstat and Imprimatur are official declarations that a book or pamphlet is free of doctrinal or moral error. No implication is contained therein that those who have granted the Nihil Obstat and Imprimatur agree with the contents, opinions or statements expressed. They do not necessarily signify that the work is approved as a basic text for catechetical instruction.

9781921946325

Cataloguing in Publication information for this title is available from the National Library of Australia.
www.nla.gov.au

The author and publisher gratefully acknowledge the permission granted to reproduce the copyright material in this book. Every effort has been made to trace copyright holders and to obtain their permission for the use of copyright material. The publisher apologises for any errors or omissions in the above list and would be grateful if notified of any corrections that should be incorporated in future reprints or editions of this book.

Garratt Publishing has included on its website a page for special notices in relation to this and our other publications.

Visit www.garrattpublishing.com.au

How to read this guide	3
When? Where? Who?	4
Who's who in the Johannine Community?	7
John and the Synoptic Gospels	9
Outline of the Gospel	11
The Prologue 1	12
The Prologue 2 Lost in Translation	14
The Prologue 3 A Gift Instead of a Gift	16
John 2 Jesus and the Temple	18
John 3 Nicodemus	20
John 4 Jesus and the Samaritan Woman	20
John 5–10 The Feasts of the Jews	23
John 5 The Sabbath	24
John 6 The Jewish Festival of Passover	25
John 7 and 8: The Feast of Tabernacles	26
John 9:1–10:22 The Blind Man Restored to Sight	28
John 10:22–42 The Festival of Dedication	29
John 11–12 The Raising of Lazarus … And Consequences	30
John 12 The Anointing and Entry to Jerusalem	31
John 13–17 The Final Discourse:	34
John 13 The Foot Washing	35
John 14 My Father's House	35
John 15–17 The Vine and the Branches:	37
John 18–19 The Hour	38
John 20 The Resurrection	41
John 21	42
Reading John Today	44

CONTENTS

HOW TO READ THIS GUIDE

When reading ancient writings like the Gospels, it is useful to have some tools to help you read with greater understanding. You need the following tools in your tool box.

A Bible with a good translation, such as the New Revised Standard Version or the New Jerusalem Bible.

As you read this guide, look up the passages and verses that are mentioned in the Gospel.

Some **background information** about the time when the Gospel was written, the composition of the local community, knowledge about its cultural and religious customs, knowledge of some of the questions and issues that this community had.

This background is particularly important when you realise that what you are reading is the way members of one community answered many of their questions about Jesus. In other words, you are reading their answers. But these answers are meaningless if you do not know their questions. For example, if I say, "the answer is 12." What question might I be asking? It could be how many months in a year? How many eggs in a dozen? How many weeks until holidays begin? Unless we know the question, the answer does not tell us much at all. So it is with the Gospels. Unless we know the questions faced by the communities at the time of the Gospel, then what we read will not make much sense to us living 2000 years later and in a very different cultural and religious context. This guide will provide you with some of the background and give you tips about where to find out more.

CURIOSITY - LOOKING FOR CLUES

A third tool that is helpful when reading any narrative, such as a Gospel, is to **recognise clues** that the writer is providing. I liken this to reading old-fashioned murder mysteries, such as an Agatha Christie novel. In these mysteries, there is often a closed group, such as 20 people on a train, or nine at a dinner party. The murder happens in chapter one, and from then on, as we read, the author provides clues as to the identity of the murderer: a light on at 3.00 am, a page torn from a diary found under the victim, etc.

The goal is that as we read we put all the clues together and when we come to the final chapter we have worked out who the culprit is. We have worked out the answer. John's Gospel needs to be read like this. The author gives us clues in every chapter and we will not get the answer until the cross. If we have followed these clues that John gives us, the story of Jesus' death will come as no surprise.

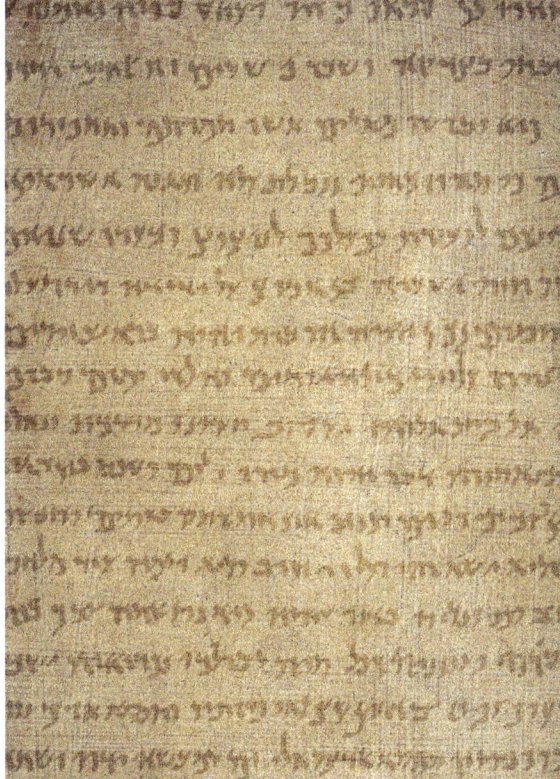

WHEN? WHERE? WHO?

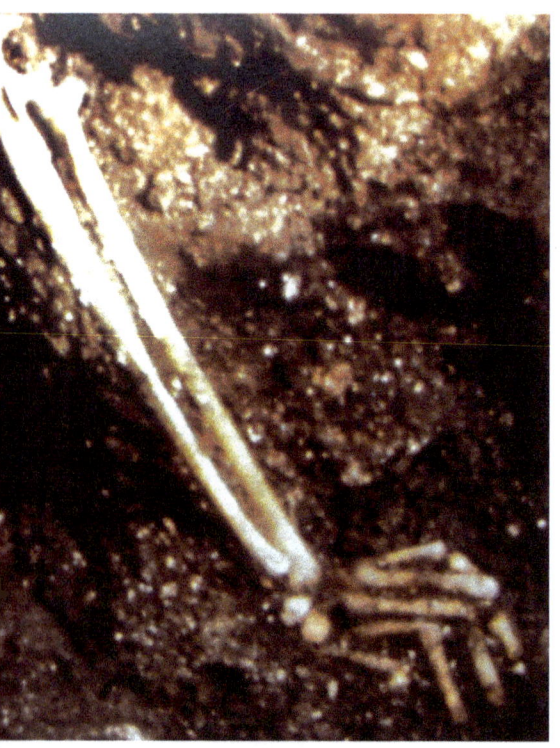

ABOVE: A REMINDER OF THE DESTRUCTION OF JERUSALEM IN 70 CE, FOUND IN THE BURNT HOUSE.

BELOW: THIS ROMAN SPEAR WAS FOUND IN THE REMAINS OF A BURNT HOUSE IN JERUSALEM.

A modern book provides us with the author's name, and information about where it was published and the date. Unfortunately, none of the Gospel manuscripts came with this precise information and so we need to look for secondary evidence such as clues in the Gospel text. Even then, often we only come up with tentative answers, or hypotheses.

WHEN?

A significant date in the first century was the year 70 CE: the Romans finally captured and destroyed Jerusalem after a four-year Jewish uprising. The destruction of Jerusalem and its Temple had major consequences for Jews and the early followers of Jesus, who at this stage were mostly Jews.

The Jerusalem Temple had been the focus of Jewish life. Its annual cycle of festivals and the daily sacrifices were important to Jews everywhere, many of whom made long pilgrimages to Jerusalem for the great festivals. Without the Temple, this rich, sacrificial and liturgical life was lost. Without the Temple, sacrifices were no longer needed, priests were not needed, and so the Jewish leadership shifted from the priests to the teachers (Rabbis). In this traumatic context, the Rabbis set about establishing a Jewish identity that could survive without the Temple. In the 80s and 90s, these Rabbis shifted the focus from Temple sacrifices to living according to Jewish Law: the Torah. It was a time for clarifying Jewish identity.

30 Jesus crucified by Romans
Time of reflection, remembering, oral preaching
50s Letters of Paul
70 Destruction of Jerusalem
Gospel of Mark
80s Gospel of Matthew
Gospel of Luke
90s Gospel of John

JESUS OR MOSES?

At this critical time, those Jews who were no longer focused on Moses and the Law but on Jesus were not welcome in Jewish synagogues. Some Jews, who were praying to Jesus, calling him *divine* and calling him Jesus the Messiah (the Christ), were considered blasphemers or heretics. The Christ-believers, nicknamed Christians, began to establish their own identity separate from Judaism. This gradual process took several centuries.

We find clues in John's Gospel that it was written in the context of such conflict about one's religious identity. Are you a follower of Moses or a follower of Jesus? Only John tells us that those who confessed Jesus as the Christ were put out of the synagogue (9:22; 12:42; 16:2). Only in John do we have Jesus clearly being given divine status when Thomas says, "My Lord and my God" (20:28). In John, there is a comparison being made between Moses and Jesus and the reader is being called to make a decision.

These are just some of the clues that led scholars to conclude that John was written in the last decade of the first century. It could not have been written much later than this as some of the earliest fragments of the Gospel have been found in Egypt and dated around 125 CE. So we date the Gospel around 95–100 CE. Also, there is an ancient tradition that this Gospel was the final Gospel.

WHO

Twice in the Gospel we read of eyewitness testimony: "An eyewitness has testified, and his testimony is true" (19:35; cf. 21:24). These affirmations of truth are linked with an anonymous character in the text known only as "the disciple whom Jesus loved" (13:23; 19:25–27; 20:3–10). There are various opinions about the identity of this Beloved Disciple. In the second century, Irenaeus, the Bishop of Lyon (c. 180–200 CE) provided us with the earliest known comments about the authorship of the Gospels. He wrote:

> MATTHEW ALSO ISSUED A WRITTEN GOSPEL AMONG THE HEBREWS IN THEIR OWN DIALECT, WHILE PETER AND PAUL WERE PREACHING AT ROME, AND LAYING THE FOUNDATIONS OF THE CHURCH. AFTER THEIR DEPARTURE, MARK, THE DISCIPLE AND INTERPRETER OF PETER, DID ALSO HAND DOWN TO US IN WRITING WHAT HAD BEEN PREACHED BY PETER. LUKE ALSO, THE COMPANION OF PAUL, RECORDED IN A BOOK THE GOSPEL PREACHED BY HIM. AFTERWARDS, JOHN, THE DISCIPLE OF THE LORD, WHO ALSO HAD LEANED UPON HIS BREAST, DID HIMSELF PUBLISH A GOSPEL DURING HIS RESIDENCE AT EPHESUS IN ASIA. (ADV. HAER. 3.1.1).

In this document, *Against Heresies*, Irenaeus attributed the last or Fourth Gospel to John, the disciple of the Lord who leaned on his breast (13:23) This *John* was identified with John, the son of Zebedee, who in the Synoptics (i.e. the Gospels of Matthew, Mark and Luke) is one of Jesus' earliest disciples (Mark 1:19) and close companion (Mark 9:2; 14:33). Many scholars today are not certain that Irenaeus was correct. In the second century, questions were being asked about which Gospels could be considered authentic; linking the Gospel to one of the original disciples may have been a strategy employed by Irenaeus to bolster its authenticity. While some people still identify him with the son of Zebedee, many scholars today prefer to consider the author as the unidentified eyewitness whose testimony and teaching are the basis for the Gospel's particular theological vision. Most commentaries will offer further details on this unresolved question.

The actual name of this ancient author seems less important than the affirmations that the Gospel is based on the eyewitness testimony of a disciple, who was with Jesus from the beginning: possibly the unnamed disciple of John the Baptist who first follows Jesus (1:35, 39). He was possibly the leader and teacher of a group of believers, passing on and shaping the memories of Jesus to meet the particular needs and circumstances of this community.

WHERE?

As we read the Gospel, there are indications that this Gospel has gone through a long process of compiling the memories of Jesus, selecting and arranging them, and presenting them in a form to emphasise Jesus' identity and mission. The Gospel has its roots in the Galilean and Judean life of Jesus. Some of the details about Jewish life, such as the stone jars of water (2:6), and the city of Jerusalem that are found only in this Gospel have been authenticated by archaeologists. While its origins were in the Jewish homeland, its final place of editing is likely to have been somewhere in the wider Greco–Roman world. Irenaeus says it was written in Ephesus, but it could have been written in any one of the larger cities in the Eastern

DID YOU KNOW?

There are a number of 'Johns' described by ancient writings:

- John, the disciple of the Lord, mentioned by Irenaeus, Bishop of Lyon (c. 180–200)
- John the Elder, mentioned by Papias, a bishop of Hierapolis in the 2nd century
- John of Patmos – the Book of Revelation claims to be written by John on the island of Patmos (Rev 1:18)
- John, son of Zebedee, the Synoptic Gospels – this John is never mentioned in the Fourth Gospel

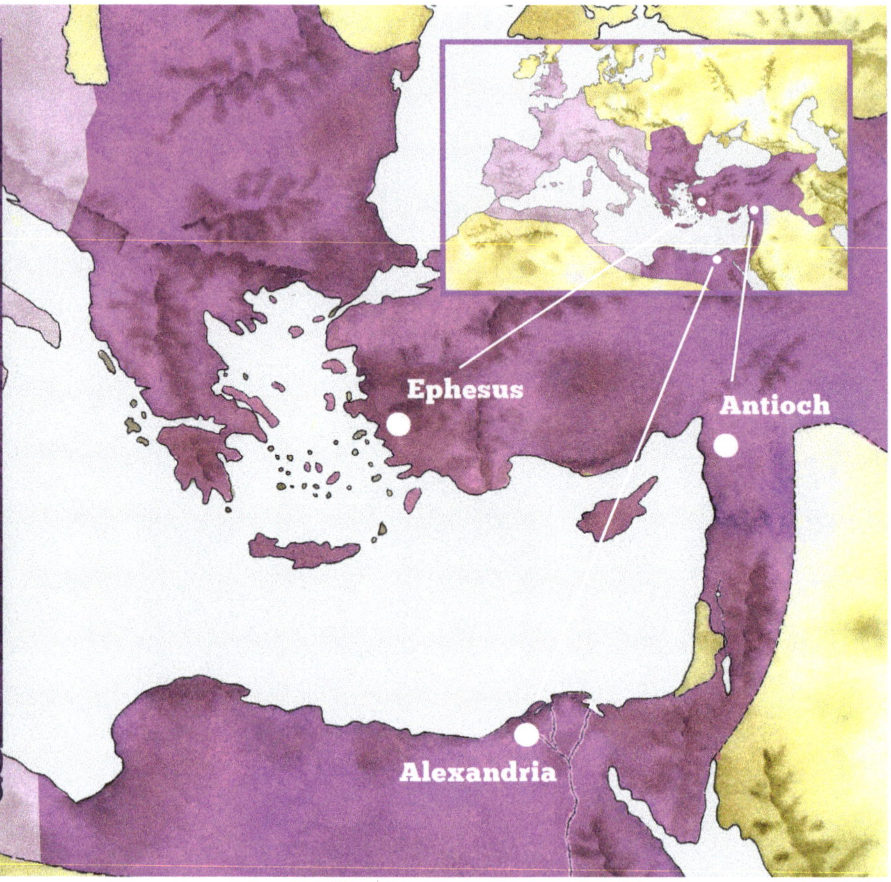

LOOKING TO JERUSALEM FROM WITHIN THE CHURCH OF DOMINUS FLEVIT (JESUS WEPT) ON MT OLIVES.

part of the Roman Empire, such as Alexandria, Antioch, or Ephesus.

WHO ARE *THE JEWS*?

In this Gospel, we have many references to characters simply called the Jews. This is very odd, since all the characters in the Gospel are Jews – with the exception of Pilate, possibly the royal official (4:46) and the Greeks who come to see Jesus (12:20). Most often the term is used to refer to the Jewish authorities associated with Jerusalem (e.g. 1:19, 2:13–22; 9:22) who are opponents of Jesus and his disciples (20:19). The term *the Jews* would never be used by a Jewish person to speak of themselves, but would be used by non-Jews, such as Pilate who asks Jesus, "Am I a Jew?" (18:35). Speaking of these characters as *the Jews*, as if everyone else is something different, distances them for the reader. 'They' are not 'us'! Many scholars today consider that this term is part of the rhetorical strategy of the Gospel, written for a community seeking its own religious identity against emerging Rabbinic Judaism.

WHO'S WHO IN THE JOHANNINE COMMUNITY?

Since the Gospel was written for a particular local community, it is helpful if we have some idea of the composition of the community and its history. The fact that Jesus' first disciples are directed to him by John the Baptist (1:29, 35–36) and that John later affirms the superiority of Jesus (3:28–30), leads scholars to believe that within this community are former disciples of John the Baptist. Chapter 4, with its narrative about the Samaritan woman and Jesus being welcomed by the Samaritan village (4:40), suggests that there are also Samaritans in the community, along with many Jews and Gentiles. Rome's destruction of Jerusalem and its Temple in 70 CE was a critical event for both Jews and Jesus' followers. Within Judaism, it brought an end to Temple worship, sacrifice, and the priesthood. Judaism from this time looked to the Law and the teaching of the Rabbis to maintain its religious identity. For the followers of Jesus, it was a time of gradually establishing a religious identity focused on Jesus and moving apart from Judaism. Both groups, Jews and Christians, also needed to negotiate living somewhere within the Roman Empire with all its civic responsibilities and Imperial cultic practices.

The practice of Judaism, with its worship, Scriptures, and festivals, is highly valued in this Gospel, and yet there is marked conflict between Jesus, as well as his disciples, with the Jewish leadership group, presented in the Gospel primarily as the Pharisees. The Gospel thus has continuity with the rich heritage of Israel. However, through its sharp polemic and negative treatment of characters called *the Jews*, it suggests we are dealing with a community whose origins were with Judaism, but who is now seeking to distance itself from the Torah-centred synagogue and affirm faith in Jesus and "life in *his* name" (20:31).

In the mid 70s, a number of Johannine scholars attempted to reconstruct the history of the development of Johannine theology, the community, and the Gospel. (Johannine is an adjective of John.) Among these hypotheses, the work of Raymond E. Brown has gained the widest acceptance.

Brown suggests four phases in the development of the community.

PHASE 1
MID 50S TO LATE 80S

An group of Jews in or near Palestine, including disciples of John the Baptist, accept Jesus, understanding him within traditional Jewish concepts as a Davidic Messiah. To this group was added a second group of Jews and Samaritans who understood Jesus in terms of a "prophet like Moses", rather than as a Davidic figure. The addition of this group led to a deeper understanding of Jesus' relationship with God, what is called a high, pre-existence Christology. These members of the community affirmed Jesus' divine status. "In the beginning was the Word, the word was with God and the Word was God" (1:1–2). This led to conflict with other Jews and eventually those believers openly confessing faith in Jesus were expelled from the synagogue (9:22; 12:42; 16:2).

PHASE 2
DURING THE 90S

By this time, the group may have moved outside the Jewish homeland into the wider Greco-Roman world, and here they began to make

DID YOU KNOW?

- The earliest scrap of manuscript is from John's Gospel. It is called Papyrus 52 (P52) and it was bought in 1920 in an Egyptian market.
- It was written in Greek capital letters and the letters were set without spaces and one line ran into the next line.

FORUSITISNOTPERMIT
TEDTOKILLANYONESOT
HATTHEWORDOFJESUSM
IGHTBEFULFILLEDWHI
CHHESPOKESIGNIFYIN
GWHATKINDOFDEATHHE
WASGOINGTODIEPILAT
EENTEREDTHEPRAETOR
IUMAGAINANDSUMMONE
DJESUSANDSAIDTOHIM
AREYOUTHEKINGOFTHE
JEWS

JOHN 18: 31–33 AND ON THE BACK 18:37–38.

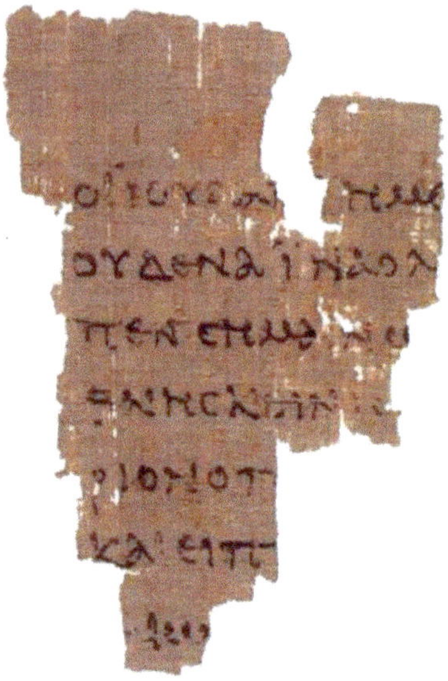

P52 APPROXIMATE DATE 125 CE.

Gentile (non-Jewish) converts. During this time, the final form of the Gospel was produced. The debates about Jesus' identity led to some within the Johannine community breaking away.

PHASE 3 C. 100

By the end of the first century, the breakaway group were placing such emphasis on the divinity of Jesus that they were losing sight of his humanity. The main group continued to emphasise the humanity of Jesus and this group is responsible for the Johannine Epistles and the strong condemnation against the breakaway group.

PHASE 4
THE SECOND CENTURY

The main group is assimilated into the broader Apostolic Church, while the breakaway group, who may have had greater numbers, moved towards heretical groups, which emphasised one aspect of Jesus so much that they lost sight of the total revelation.

It is important to realise that this is a hypothetical reconstruction of the Johannine community based on the writing found in the Gospels and Epistles attributed to 'John'.

A FRIENDLY GUIDE TO JOHN'S GOSPEL

JOHN AND THE SYNOPTIC GOSPELS

John contains fewer miracles than the Synoptic Gospels, but those included in John are dramatic. In John, these miracles are named *signs*, which emphasises that these events point to a deeper meaning. They are meant to lead to a deeper perception of Jesus' identity. Often these *signs* are accompanied by long discourses spoken by Jesus to bring out the underlying meaning of these signs. Where the Synoptics describe a single journey from Galilee to Jerusalem across one year, in John's Gospel Jesus travels back and forth between Galilee and Jerusalem several times. John mentions three Passover Festivals, which means that Jesus' ministry was at least two, if not three years, which is probably more accurate. Why is John so different?

All the Gospels have their basis in the historical memory of Jesus: what sort of man he was, what he did, how he lived, what he taught. In the years after his death, these memories were shared and shaped by Jesus' early followers, but communities might emphasise different aspects of these memories. A community composed mainly of Jewish believers might emphasis Jesus the great teacher like Moses. A community that was predominantly Gentile (non-Jews) might emphasise Jesus' association with outsiders, such as tax collectors, the poor and sinners.

Eventually these oral stories were collected, shaped, and written. Mark is the earliest of these written documents to have survived, written probably around the year 70 CE.

The next two Gospels, Matthew and Luke, follow Mark's outline and often copy Mark, so they

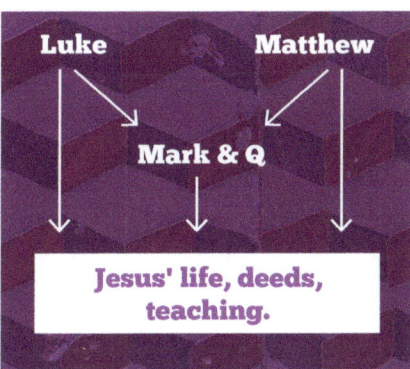

obviously have a written copy of his Gospel to use as a source for their own Gospel. It is likely they also had another shared document (scholars call this Q: short for the word Source/Quelle in German) and other distinct traditions which they drew on. This means that the first three Gospels are similar. They have a similar perspective or vision (hence syn-optic) on the life of Jesus.

When we turn to John's Gospel, this author does not follow Mark's pattern, nor does he provide any of the parables found in the Synoptics, nor have any exorcisms. Some of the episodes he recounts are in the Synoptic Gospels (such as the feeding of the great crowd, Jesus' driving the animals from the Temple and the anointing), but

DID YOU KNOW?

- **Some of the information John gives us about Jerusalem has been found by archaeologists to be historically accurate. John seems to know the location of Caiaphas's house and the *praetorium* (18:28). The Pool of Siloam (John 9) was recently discovered south of the Temple Mount.**

- **In John 5, there is a description of a pool where people gathered for healing. John describes it as having five porticos. There is such a pool found just outside the Temple and it appears to have a long history as a place of healing, even prior to Roman times.**

many episodes are unique to John: changing water to wine at Cana, speaking with a Samaritan woman, raising Lazarus from the tomb. While his Gospel is different, the details that John provides and what we learn about Jewish practices and festivals when the Temple still existed both match archaeological discoveries. So John, even though different, is also drawing on the same bedrock of traditional Jesus material, but selecting and shaping this material differently. We could add John to the above diagram like this:

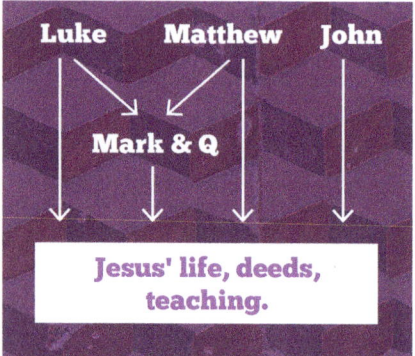

THE POOL OF BETHESDA WITH FIVE PORTICOS.

OUTLINE OF THE GOSPEL

HINT: HAVE YOUR GOSPEL OPEN SO YOU CAN FOLLOW THE TEXTS AND VERSES MENTIONED.

In his 1966 commentary on the Gospel of John, Raymond E. Brown divided the Gospel into two major sections:

1. Chapters 1:19–12:50, which he designated the "Book of Signs". These chapters concern Jesus' miracles, which in this Gospel are called "signs" (e.g. 2:11; 4:54).

2. Chapters 13:1–20:31, which he named the "Book of Glory". These chapters focus on Jesus' return to the Father, which in this Gospel is called his glorification (e.g. 13:31, 14:13; 17:1, 5, 24).

According to Brown, these two major sections are introduced by a Prologue (1:1–18) and concluded with an Epilogue (21:1–25).

Within the Book of Signs, smaller subdivisions are suggested by the text. Chapter 1 presents a sequence of days (designated by the repeated phrase, "the next day" – 1:29, 35, 43) beginning with the ministry of John (1:19–34) and concluding with Jesus' promise to his disciples that they would see "greater things" (1:50–51). Chapter 2 begins in "Cana in Galilee" (2:1) and the changing of the water into wine is called "the first of his signs" (2:11). At the end of chapter 4, the narrative returns to "Cana in Galilee" (4:46) and the cure of the royal official's son is called "the second sign". These repetitions suggest that chapters 2, 3 and 4 are a literary unit, which Brown and others call "From Cana to Cana".

The next six chapters all deal with issues linked to specific Jewish feasts and are introduced with the phrase, "the feast of the Jews": the Sabbath (5:1, 9), Passover (6:4), Tabernacles (7:2), and Dedication (10:22).

Chapters 11 and 12 focus on the person of Lazarus, his death and resurrection (11:1–44) and its consequences for Jesus (11:45–53; 12:10, 17–19). The death and raising of Lazarus makes a transition from Jesus' public ministry to the final chapters – his final meal (13:2), teaching his disciples the meaning of his departure (Chaps 13–16), Jesus' prayer to his Father (Ch. 17), and his own death (Chaps 18–19) and resurrection (Ch. 20). Many scholars today consider that

The Gospel outline can be set out as follows.

1:1–18	Prologue

The Book of Signs (Jesus' public ministry)

1:19–51	The First Days
2:1–4:54	Cana to Cana
5:1–10:42	The Feasts of the Jews
11:1–12:50	Transition: Lazarus: A story of death and resurrection

The Book of Glory (Jesus with his own)

13:1–17:26	The Farewell Discourse
18:1–19:42	The Passion
20:1–29	The Resurrection
20:31–31	Conclusion
21:1–24	Epilogue (editorial addition)
21:25	Editorial conclusion

> **DID YOU KNOW?**
> - Each of the Evangelists has a symbol. Because of its lofty vision of Jesus, John's symbol is the eagle.

the Gospel, at least in its earlier form, concluded with a brief statement of its purpose (20:30–31). Chapter 21 appears to be an early editor's addition to the original text, an Epilogue, which then has its own conclusion (21:24–25). This chapter establishes Peter as the pastoral leader of the group and explains that the death of the Beloved Disciple is not to be a cause of concern.

THE PROLOGUE 1

When you go to a ballet or musical, the work opens with the orchestra playing an introduction to the main musical themes. Similarly, the Gospel of John opens with a Prologue (1:1–18) that introduces the reader to the major themes of the Gospel: who Jesus was, what his mission was, how people responded to him.

 The Prologue begins with the opening words of the Book of Genesis, "In the beginning…" This is a clue to alert the reader to a major theme of this Gospel: life. Later in the narrative Jesus will say, "I have come that you may have life in abundance" (10:10). He will frequently speak of a gift he offers which he names *eternity-life*. Most translations will say, "eternal life", but I prefer to speak of "eternity-life" to emphasise that Jesus is not just offering ordinary life extended

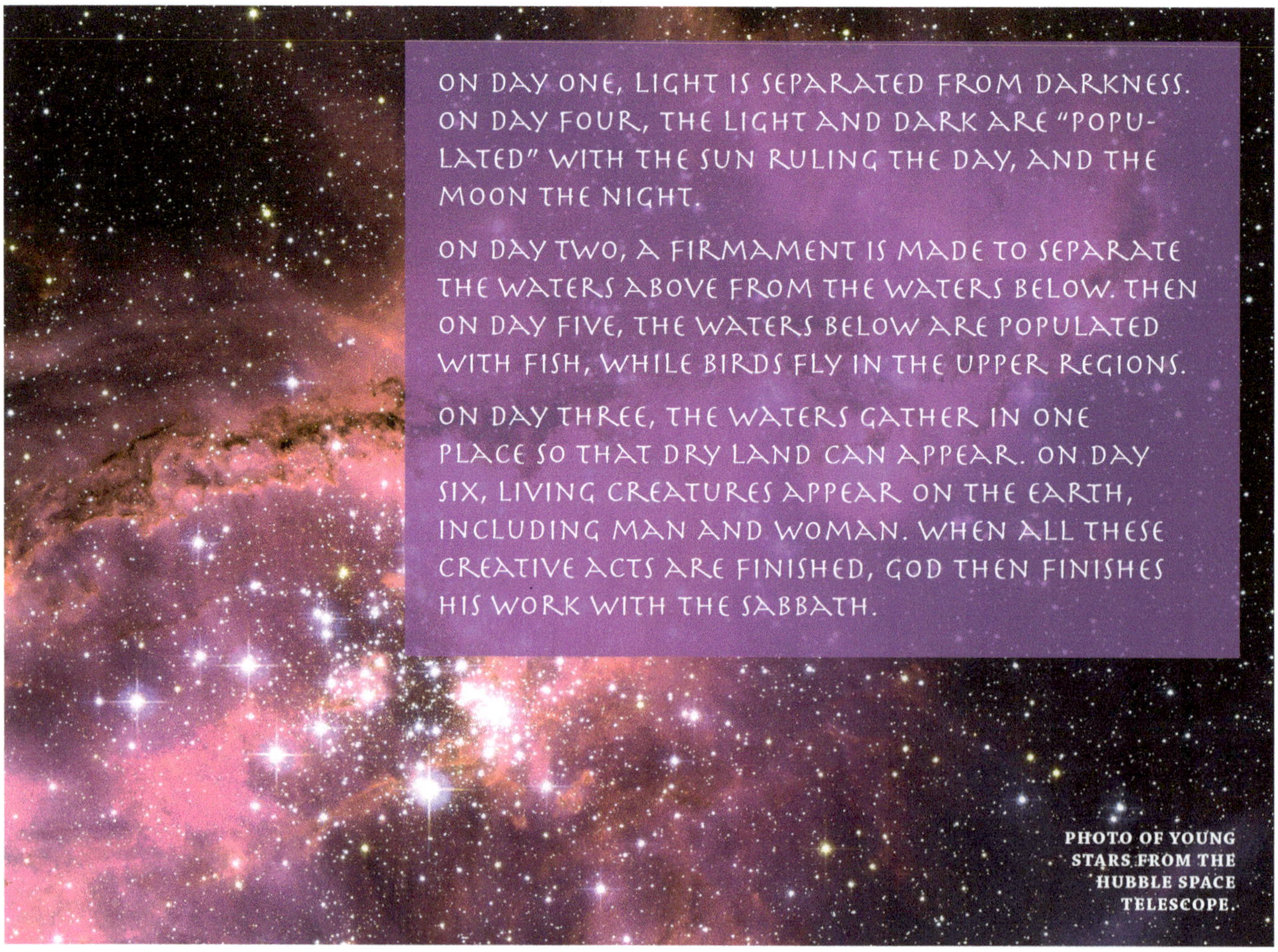

> ON DAY ONE, LIGHT IS SEPARATED FROM DARKNESS. ON DAY FOUR, THE LIGHT AND DARK ARE "POPULATED" WITH THE SUN RULING THE DAY, AND THE MOON THE NIGHT.
>
> ON DAY TWO, A FIRMAMENT IS MADE TO SEPARATE THE WATERS ABOVE FROM THE WATERS BELOW. THEN ON DAY FIVE, THE WATERS BELOW ARE POPULATED WITH FISH, WHILE BIRDS FLY IN THE UPPER REGIONS.
>
> ON DAY THREE, THE WATERS GATHER IN ONE PLACE SO THAT DRY LAND CAN APPEAR. ON DAY SIX, LIVING CREATURES APPEAR ON THE EARTH, INCLUDING MAN AND WOMAN. WHEN ALL THESE CREATIVE ACTS ARE FINISHED, GOD THEN FINISHES HIS WORK WITH THE SABBATH.

PHOTO OF YOUNG STARS FROM THE HUBBLE SPACE TELESCOPE.

in time, but a whole new quality of life – the life that God lives in eternity.

One way of understanding ancient writing is to try to determine the writer's method of structuring his work. When scholars examine the Prologue, they come up with various suggestions for its structure. I think this evangelist, let's call him John, has based the Prologue on the opening chapter of Genesis. If you look at Genesis 1, you will see it has an introduction (Gen 1:1–3), then the seven days of creation, then a one sentence conclusion (Gen 2:4a: "These are the generations of the heavens and the earth when they were created"). The seven days of creation are set out in two parallel groups of three stanzas, leading to the seventh day.

If you look carefully at the pattern of the Creation story and the Prologue, you will notice one major difference: in the Prologue there is no Sabbath day of rest. This is another clue to understanding John's story of Jesus. The Gospel understands that God's work of creation was not finished "in the beginning". God is still working, and in fact Jesus' mission, which this Gospel calls his "work", is to do God's work and bring creation to its completion. Jesus says, "My Father is still working, and I am working" (5:17). It is only on the Cross that this Gospel announces that the work of creation is completed, when Jesus says, "It is finished" (19:30). Then, just as in Genesis, we are told that the next day was the Sabbath (19:31).

This first creation narrative can be set out like this:

Introduction: *In the beginning . . .* (Gen 1:1-3)

Day 1 Light and darkness	Day 4 Sun, moon and stars
Day 2 Waters above and waters below	Day 5 Fish and birds
Day 3 Land and sea	Day 6 Land animals, man, and woman

Day 7 The work is finished – the Sabbath.

Conclusion: *These are the generations of the heavens and earth.* (Gen 2:4a)

I believe the Prologue to John's Gospel follows this same pattern.

Introduction: *In the beginning . . .* (vv 1-3)

Stanza 1 Light/darkness (vv 4-5)	Stanza 4 We saw his glory (v 14)
Stanza 2 John's witness (vv 6-8)	Stanza 5 John's witness (v 15)
Stanza 3 Two responses to the Word (vv 9-13)	Stanza 6 Two gifts: Moses and Jesus (vv 16-17)

Conclusion: The Son and Father (v 18)

In these subtle ways, John presents his story of Jesus as bringing to completion God's work of creation. The Prologue offers hints of this theme, which the Gospel will then develop.

ALLUSIONS

New Testament writers frequently make allusions to Old Testament texts that their audience would instantly recall. The same thing happens with popular films. One line from a film can recall the entire film: who were the characters, the actors, what it was about, etc.

What movie do you think of when you read these lines?

"Go ahead . . ."
"The Force . . ."
"Frankly my dear . . ."
"Gooood morning Vietnam . . ."

Film makers can also allude to earlier films through using memorable images, such as Rocky standing on the top step of the Art Museum of Philadelphia, and musical scores, such as Chariots of Fire, or Star Wars.

The major script the New Testament authors had, which they knew their audience would know, was the Old Testament. The Gospel has many allusions to the Old Testament, so readers today need to be alert for echoes and allusions from Israel's Scriptures.

A FRIENDLY GUIDE TO JOHN'S GOSPEL

THE PROLOGUE 2
LOST IN TRANSLATION

The Prologue also draws upon two other major Old Testament images: those of the Temple and Divine Wisdom. Because we are reading in English, some of these images get lost in translation.

The Prologue begins with the image of God's Word (*Logos*) with God at the beginning of creation. Creation is made through the Word, and the Word was in the world, but was not known (v 9). Then in verse 14 we read, "The Word became flesh and dwelt among us". The word *dwelt* is actually the Greek word for a tent and is the word found in the Old Testament to speak of the Tabernacle. John's original audience/readers would have heard these allusions to the Tabernacle. John is recalling the long tradition of God coming to dwell with Israel in the Ark of the Covenant, which was a box to carry the stone tablets of the Ten Commandments.

The Ark was housed in an elaborate Tent, called the Tabernacle, which moved with the people on their journey. This sacred object was the symbol for God's presence among them. Later, when the people settled down, Solomon built a magnificent Temple in Jerusalem to house the Ark. The Temple then became the symbol of God's presence dwelling with Israel. The Temple was even called the Lord's house.

So when John writes, "The Word became flesh and *tabernacled* among us," he recalls Israel's story and says to his community that in Jesus, God is now dwelling in our midst, as God once dwelt in the midst of Israel.

Later in Israel's history, they began to consider and wonder about the world around them. They saw orderly patterns in the cycle of the seasons, in the pattern of days and nights, and the four-weekly cycle of the moon. They attributed this marvellous order in creation to God's Wisdom. They spoke of Wisdom being with God in the beginning; they personified wisdom and spoke of her as a darling child (the Hebrew text is unclear and the word could also be a craftsman), working beside God in the act of creation.

THE LORD CREATED ME [WISDOM] AT THE BEGINNING, THE FIRST OF GOD'S ACTS OF LONG AGO.

AGES AGO I WAS SET UP, AT THE FIRST, BEFORE THE BEGINNING OF THE EARTH.

WHEN THERE WERE NO DEPTHS, I WAS BROUGHT FORTH, WHEN THERE WERE NO SPRINGS ABOUNDING WITH WATER.

BEFORE THE MOUNTAINS HAD BEEN SHAPED, BEFORE THE HILLS, I WAS BROUGHT FORTH—

WHEN GOD ESTABLISHED THE HEAVENS, I WAS THERE, WHEN THE FOUNTAINS OF THE DEEP WERE ESTABLISHED,

THERE I WAS, LIKE A DARLING CHILD (OR CRAFTSMAN) AND I WAS GOD'S DAILY DELIGHT,

REJOICING BEFORE GOD ALWAYS,

REJOICING IN THE INHABITED WORLD AND DELIGHTING IN THE HUMAN RACE.

PROVERBS 8:22-31

IMAGE OF THE ARK FROM AN ANCIENT SYNAGOGUE IN CAPERNAUM.

Divine Wisdom became a way of speaking of God being present, here, in this world.

In the book of Sirach, one of the last Old Testament books to be written, Divine Wisdom speaks of looking for a place to dwell, and then finding a resting place among the people of Israel. Just as Wisdom created order in creation, she also created an orderly way of human living, and this order was thought to be expressed in Israel's Law, the Torah.

> WISDOM PRAISES HERSELF, AND TELLS OF HER GLORY IN THE MIDST OF HER PEOPLE.
>
> "I CAME FORTH FROM THE MOUTH OF THE MOST HIGH, AND COVERED THE EARTH LIKE A MIST.
>
> I DWELT IN THE HIGHEST HEAVENS, AND MY THRONE WAS IN A PILLAR OF CLOUD.
>
> OVER WAVES OF THE SEA, OVER ALL THE EARTH, AND OVER EVERY PEOPLE AND NATION I HAVE HELD SWAY.
>
> AMONG ALL THESE, I SOUGHT A RESTING PLACE; IN WHOSE TERRITORY SHOULD I ABIDE?
>
> THEN THE CREATOR OF ALL THINGS GAVE ME A COMMAND, AND MY CREATOR CHOSE THE PLACE FOR MY TENT.
>
> SAYING, 'MAKE YOUR DWELLING IN JACOB, AND IN ISRAEL RECEIVE YOUR INHERITANCE.'
>
> BEFORE THE AGES, IN THE BEGINNING, I WAS CREATED, AND FOR ALL THE AGES, I SHALL NOT CEASE TO BE.
>
> IN THE HOLY TENT, I MINISTERED BEFORE GOD, AND SO I WAS ESTABLISHED IN ZION.
>
> THUS IN THE BELOVED CITY GOD GAVE ME A RESTING PLACE, AND IN JERUSALEM WAS MY DOMAIN.
>
> ALL THIS IS THE BOOK OF THE COVENANT OF THE MOST HIGH GOD, THE LAW THAT MOSES COMMANDED US
>
> AS AN INHERITANCE FOR THE CONGREGATIONS OF JACOB.
>
> **SIRACH 24: 1-11, 23**

First-century Jews would hear in John's Prologue allusions to these Old Testament writings. Making use of these Old Testament images, John's Gospel affirms that Divine Wisdom, who was with God in the beginning, creating order in the world, has now found a resting place, and has pitched her tent in human history. Jesus is the incarnation of Divine Wisdom, and this community bears witness to their experience.

> WHO HAS GONE UP INTO HEAVEN, AND TAKEN HER [WISDOM], AND BROUGHT HER DOWN FROM THE CLOUDS?
>
> NO ONE KNOWS THE WAY TO HER,
>
> OR IS CONCERNED ABOUT THE PATH TO HER.
>
> BUT THE ONE WHO KNOWS ALL THINGS KNOWS HER,
>
> GOD FOUND HER THROUGH UNDERSTANDING.
>
> THE ONE WHO PREPARED THE EARTH FOR ALL TIME
>
> FILLED IT WITH FOUR-FOOTED CREATURES;
>
> THE ONE WHO SENDS FORTH THE LIGHT, AND IT GOES;
>
> GOD CALLED IT, AND IT OBEYED, TREMBLING;
>
> THE STARS SHONE IN THEIR WATCHES, AND WERE GLAD;
>
> GOD CALLED THEM, AND THEY SAID, "HERE WE ARE!"
>
> THEY SHONE WITH GLADNESS FOR THE ONE WHO MADE THEM.
>
> BARUCH 3:29–34

THUS IN THE BELOVED CITY GOD GAVE ME A RESTING PLACE, AND IN JERUSALEM WAS MY DOMAIN.

DID YOU KNOW?

- The word 'Wisdom' in Hebrew is feminine in its form – Hokmah. In Greek also it is feminine – Sophia.

THE PROLOGUE 3
A GIFT INSTEAD OF A GIFT

The Prologue tells the story of the Word who from the beginning is in loving union with God, then the Word is present in the world (Gk. *kosmos*), but the world did not know this. Verse 11 states, "He came to his own" (*eis ta idia*); this is understood to refer to the people of Israel. As the Gospel will show, some of his own people rejected him and collaborated with Rome to have Jesus crucified. This was one response.

 But, there was another response. Some of his own did receive him, they believed in him and the Prologue says that those who accepted him received a gift, described as the authority, or the right, "to become children of God" (v 12). These were the two reactions experienced by the Word. In the first three stanzas, the story of the Word coming into the world and the world's reaction is reported in the third person. At verse 14, a change happens. In the second group of three stanzas we hear the story in first person testimony: the Word dwelt among "us"; "we" saw his glory (v 14). Then John speaks in his own voice, "This was he of whom 'I' said" (v 15).

The last stanza describes two contrasting gifts: "From his fullness, we have all received a gift instead of a gift" (v 16). If you look at your translation it probably reads "grace upon grace". This is not a good translation. The Greek says, *charis anti charitos*. The word *charis* is like the English word *charism*, or *charismatic*, meaning a gifted individual. The word *anti* normally means 'against' or 'opposed to'. So the verse really presents two gifts – and compares them – one gift instead of another. The next verse identifies these two gifts, "For the Law was given through Moses". This was Israel's great gift. But the Gospel asserts an even greater gift, "the true gift came through Jesus Christ" (v 17). The gift Jesus offers is not described here but is described in the parallel section. What Jesus gives is "the right to become children of God".

The Prologue thus tells the reader the overall plot of the Gospel. As readers, we know what is going to happen. When we move into the Gospel narrative, we watch the characters in the story, who do not have this information, as they respond to Jesus. How will they choose? Will they choose to stay with the Mosaic gift of the Law, or will they be open to Jesus?

JESUS' MINISTRY BEGINS

John's Gospel starts the ministry of Jesus with John the Baptist and the gathering of the first few disciples. John provides us with what is probably accurate historical information: that some of Jesus' first disciples, and even Jesus himself, were at first disciples of John.

'CANA TO CANA'

 As noted in the Outline, chapter 2 begins in "Cana in Galilee" (2:1) and at the end of chapter 4 the narrative returns to "Cana in Galilee" (4:46). The abundance of wine in chapter 2 is called the "first sign" and the cure of the royal official's son in chapter 4 is called "the

second sign". These repetitions are clues that chapters 2, 3 and 4 are a literary unit, commonly known as "From Cana to Cana".

One approach to interpreting this section is to focus on the way the characters in the text respond to Jesus. In chapters 2 and 3, the characters are Jews, while in chapter 4 the narrative moves outside Judaism into the world of Samaritans (4:1–42) and the Gentile official (4:46–54). Within the world of Judaism, the first significant character is the mother of Jesus. In spite of Jesus' retort, his mother directs the servants to "do whatever he tells you" (2:5). She trusts Jesus' words and her trust leads to the bountiful supply of wine. She displays authentic faith in Jesus – at least in terms of this Gospel. With the mother of Jesus as a model, the reader then meets other Jewish characters to evaluate their faith response to Jesus: firstly the Jews in the Temple (2:13–22), then Nicodemus (2:23–3:10), and then John the Baptist (3:25–30). The Jews in the Temple are portrayed as completely rejecting Jesus' words (2:20): they display no faith in him. Nicodemus comes to Jesus (3:2), but fails to comprehend his words (3:4, 9) and so, at this point in the Gospel, he can be described as having partial faith. Following Nicodemus (2:23–3:10), John the Baptist testifies about Jesus that "he must increase; I must decrease" (3:30). These words, and John's recognising Jesus as the bridegroom (3:29), indicate that John has perfect faith. So there is a sequence: no faith ('the Jews'), partial faith (Nicodemus), perfect faith (John the Baptist), with the sequence introduced by a model of perfect faith in the mother of Jesus. The narrative then moves beyond the world of Judaism and shows a similar faith journey.

In the narrative of the Samaritan Woman (4:1–42), note the gradual shift in her attitude towards Jesus. At first, she is dismissive of him: "You, a Jew, ask me, a Samaritan, for a drink?" (4:9). She shows no faith. But as the conversation continues her attitude changes and she addresses him as "sir" and requests water from him (4:11, 15). At this stage, she is showing partial faith. Then she considers him a prophet (4:19), and finally, the Messiah/Christ (4:25). Now she shows full faith and she leaves Jesus to go and bring other villagers to him, and they also come to acknowledge Jesus as the "Saviour of the World" (4:42). This one story shows a complete journey, from no faith, to partial faith, to complete faith.

Chapter 4 concludes back in Cana with an official, whom most believe to be a Gentile, who also shows complete faith when he trusts Jesus' word that his son will live (4:50). Like the mother of Jesus, this official is at first rebuffed by Jesus (4:48), but he too persists and his faith is rewarded. This Gentile official and the mother of Jesus serve as models of perfect Johannine faith. These two characters are like bookends; between these two characters, the reader is introduced to others, both within and beyond Judaism, who display various faith responses to Jesus: full faith, partial faith, no faith. The evangelist has crafted his narrative in this way to invite all hearers/readers into their own journey of faith, be they Jews, Samaritans, or Gentiles.

THE JORDAN ENTERING THE SEA OF GALILEE.

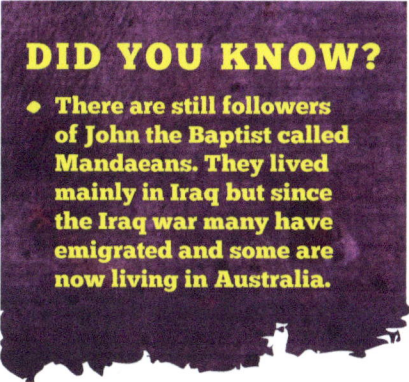

DID YOU KNOW?

- There are still followers of John the Baptist called Mandaeans. They lived mainly in Iraq but since the Iraq war many have emigrated and some are now living in Australia.

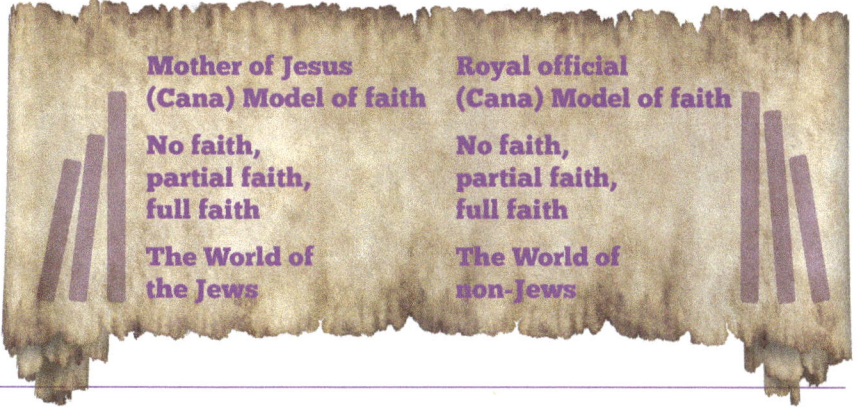

Mother of Jesus (Cana) Model of faith

No faith, partial faith, full faith

The World of the Jews

Royal official (Cana) Model of faith

No faith, partial faith, full faith

The World of non-Jews

A FRIENDLY GUIDE TO JOHN'S GOSPEL

A LARGE CLAY JAR FROM MASADA LIKE THE KIND OF JARS THAT WOULD HAVE BEEN FILLED WITH WINE AT THE WEDDING AT CANA.

DID YOU KNOW?
- John's Gospel was called the 'Spiritual' Gospel by Clement of Alexandria (c. 200), because John frequently makes use of symbols and allusions pointing to a deeper meaning.

MORE TO IT THAN MEETS THE EYE

The Gospel was written for an audience living towards the end of the first century familiar with the traditions and Scriptures of Israel, and the writer frequently communicates the deeper meaning of his narratives using key symbols. Today's readers need help to understand these symbols. Frequently the Gospel depends on the reader knowing an Old Testament text, either explicitly quoted (e.g. 2:17; 6:31 etc.), or just alluded to (e.g. 1:51 and its allusion to Gen 28:12). Often the reader is expected to know Jewish customs (e.g. foot washing) or the rituals and symbols associated with Jewish festivals. Without this knowledge, the modern reader can miss the major point of a Johannine episode.

Take for example, the first miracle at Cana (2:1–12). At first glance, it appears to be a simple miracle story: Jesus provides abundant wine at a wedding. But a closer reading reveals far more. The steward of the feast called the bridegroom to congratulate him on the provision of such abundant good wine towards the end of the feast (2:9–10). This indicates that the bridegroom at a Jewish wedding ceremony had the task of providing the wine. But, in this case, it was Jesus who provided the wine and so the evangelist is giving a clue, or a sign, that Jesus is the real bridegroom at this feast. Within the Old Testament, the image of a bridegroom and bride was frequently used to speak of the loving relationship between God and Israel (Hos 2:19–24; Jer 2:2) and a feast was a symbol of the covenant (Exod 24:9–11; Isa 25:6–9).

This miracle begins with the words "on the third day" (2:1) and concludes with the statement that this was the first sign when Jesus "revealed his glory" (2:11). These phrases, "the third day", "revealed his glory", echo the language found in Exodus 19 when Israel arrived at Mount Sinai and entered into the solemn covenant with God. At Sinai the people were told to prepare "for the third day" (Exod 19:11x2, 15, 16), for on the third day God's glory was to be revealed (Exod 19:16). The evangelist presumes that his audience is familiar with this important Old Testament text and so will understand the allusion, not unlike today when a line from a movie will immediately evoke the entire film. The first miracle at Cana, when read within this Exodus context, opens up a richer understanding of the narrative. Jesus is being presented as the covenanting God of Israel, the loving bridegroom providing abundant wine for the wedding feast. This example illustrates that one will read with deeper understanding if one has a commentary as a guide.

JOHN 2 JESUS AND THE TEMPLE

Cana is in the Northern region near the Sea of Galilee. The next scene has Jesus in the South, in Jerusalem, around the Feast of Passover. All the Gospels record the dramatic actions of Jesus in the Jerusalem Temple when he drives out the animals and overturns the tables of the money changers. As 21st-century Christians, we are probably shocked that the buying and selling of animals and money changing was taking place in the Temple, which is why many refer to this scene as "the Cleansing in the

Temple". But if you were a first-century Jew, having these things in the Temple before Passover was normal and in fact was a help to celebrating the festival.

Passover was one of the three major Jewish festivals when adult males were expected to come to Jerusalem to celebrate the feast. Pilgrims came from all parts of the Empire, and in order to celebrate Passover they needed a lamb to sacrifice. In order to help the thousands who came from distant regions, lambs were available. Also, because so many came to this festival, this was a time when Jews brought money to pay for the upkeep of the Temple and its sacrifices. This was called the annual Temple tax. But this tax could not be paid with ordinary coins from the Empire since these coins had a portrait of the Emperor calling him "divine". To the Jews this was blasphemy. The Jews therefore had special permission to mint their own coins without this image of Caesar. When the pilgrims arrived in Jerusalem, they had to change their Roman coins for special Jewish coins before they could pay their Temple tax. For this reason, the priests permitted tables to be set up in the outer courts of the Temple for a month before Passover. The money changers and animals were all a necessary part of preparing for the great festival. Jesus was not "cleansing" the Temple! His actions had a far deeper meaning. In driving out the animals, and overturning the tables used for collecting the Temple tax, in effect Jesus was saying: "this Temple system is over. This is no longer the way to be in relationship with God."

 In John's Gospel, after his temple actions, Jesus is confronted by the Jewish authorities asking him for a sign of his authority to act as he did. They seemed to have understood the deeper meaning of his deed. In John, Jesus replies with a cryptic statement: "Destroy this Temple and in three days I will raise it up" (2:19). The Jews think he is talking about the Temple building and reject his words scornfully. The scene ends here for the characters. But the evangelist then gives the readers additional information – "He spoke of the Temple of his body" (2:21). Because the readers have read the Prologue they should understand this, for the Prologue had introduced Jesus as the tabernacle. "The Word became flesh and dwelt/tabernacled among us" (1:14). Jesus is the dwelling place of God. The Temple, and its sacrificial system, is no longer needed.

 Note that in this chapter, the Temple, called in the Old Testament the *Lord's* house, Jesus renames as "my *Father's* house". This will be very important later in the text.

The scene shows two responses to Jesus. The authorities reject his words. But his disciples continue to follow him. The narrator suggests that at the time of the incident they had no more understanding of him than the authorities and it was only after his death and resurrection that they remembered and came to understand. "When therefore he was raised from the dead, his disciples remembered that he had said this; and they believed the scriptures and the word which Jesus had spoken" (2:22). Even without fully understanding, they continued to trust his words.

A MODEL OF THE TEMPLE AT THE TIME OF JESUS. THE LARGE OUTER COURT WOULD HAVE BEEN WHERE THE TABLES FOR THE MONEY-CHANGERS, AND THE COLLECTION OF THE TEMPLE-TAX. GENTILES WERE PERMITTED IN THESE OUTER COURTS, WHILE ONLY JEWS WERE PERMITTED THROUGH THE GOLDEN GATE TO THE INNER SANCTUARY.

Chapter 2 has provided the reader with two major images of Jesus that provide insight into his identity: Jesus is the bridegroom, an image of the Old Testament God of Israel's covenant; and Jesus is a living Temple of God's presence. These are major clues that the reader needs in order to understand the rest of this Gospel.

This is the most ancient existing map of Jerusalem, created with mosaic tiles on the floor of a Church in Madaba (modern day Jordan).

It shows two main streets from the Damascus gate on the left. On the lower street, the large building in the centre is the basilica built by Constantine in the 4th Century to enclose the site of Golgotha and the Tomb of the resurrection.

Greek: ☐☐☐☐☐ ΙΙ☐☐☐C
☐☐☐☐C☐☐☐☐

HOLY CITY JERUSALEM

JOHN 3 NICODEMUS

Chapter 3 introduces another Jewish leader called Nicodemus. He accepts Jesus as a teacher, but then cannot grasp what Jesus means by being "born again" (3:3, 5). Jesus then speaks of two types of birth: ordinary human birth through water, when a mother's waters break, and a second birth of the Spirit. This is what Jesus means by being "born again": a spiritual birth. Nicodemus keeps wondering, "How is this possible?" (3:4, 9). While he does not totally reject Jesus' words, his lack of understanding means he cannot accept them at this time. Nicodemus' journey of faith will continue in chapter 7, and then he will re-appear to help bury Jesus (19:39).

This Jewish section finishes with John the Baptist declaring the superiority of Jesus. He uses the image from a wedding and speaks of Jesus as the bridegroom, while he is only the bridegroom's friend, or "best man". "He who has the bride is the bridegroom; the bridegroom's friend, who stands and hears him, rejoices greatly at the bridegroom's voice; therefore this joy of mine has been made full. He must increase, but I must decrease" (3:29–30).

I suggest you re-read chapters 2 and 3, alert now to its deeper meaning and the symbols of Jesus' identity as the bridegroom and Temple. These symbols will be important to understand chapter 4.

JOHN 4 JESUS AND THE SAMARITAN WOMAN

Before looking at John 4, there is critical background information you need so you will be able to understand the deeper symbols and storyline running through this episode.

BOY MEETS GIRL AT THE LOCAL!

In the Old Testament, a well was a frequent, even typical, meeting place for a young man to find his future bride. Isaac's wife, Rebekah, was found at a well (Gen 24:10–33), Jacob met Rachel (Gen 29:1–14), and Moses met Zipporah at wells (Exod 2:15–22). The story of Jacob meeting Rachel is particularly important because the well in John 4 is called Jacob's well. Jacob met Rachel in the middle of the day, which is the same time that Jesus meets the Samaritan woman (John 4:6). The opening verses of John 4 locating Jesus at Jacob's well in the middle of the day, then meeting a woman, naturally raise an expectation that this meeting is going to lead to a marriage. But remember, marriage is the great symbol of God's covenant with the people of Israel; the covenant is a spiritual marriage.

TEMPLE AND CREATION

Within Judaism, the Temple was thought to be the place where all the waters of creation had their origin. It is the meeting place between heaven and earth. Jerusalem was even called the earth's navel (Ezek 38:12; translated as 'centre'). It was thought that the altar of the Jerusalem Temple rested over the great chasm leading down to the primeval waters of Creation, waters that in the time of Noah gushed up to flood the earth. Ezekiel 47 depicts this mythology of life-giving streams of water flowing from the Temple. When Jesus, who has identified himself as the Temple, comes to Samaria, and sits upon the well, all this creation and water imagery comes to the fore. Jesus, as the Temple, is able to offer the life-giving waters of creation.

JEWS AND SAMARITANS

When the people of Israel first settled in the land, they were organised in 12 tribes. Around the year 1000 BCE, David united all the tribes into one kingdom, which he passed on to his son Solomon. In the time of Solomon's sons, the kingdom was divided into two nations. Ten of the tribes in the North broke away from a hereditary model of kinship and formed their own nation with its capital city Samaria. Two tribes stayed with David's line of Kings and the capital, Jerusalem. In time, the Northern Kingdom was defeated (721 BCE), and, as was the custom, many of the people were deported and foreigners were brought into the land. The resulting intermarriage of the original Israelites and foreigners led to the group called the Samaritans. Other Jews considered Samaritans a mixed race and had nothing to do with them.

Two hundred years after this time, the prophet Ezekiel looked to the future when God would re-unite the people and form them into one nation again.

THE WORD OF THE LORD CAME TO ME: TAKE A STICK AND WRITE ON IT, "FOR JUDAH, AND THE ISRAELITES ASSOCIATED WITH IT" (this was the Southern Kingdom); THEN TAKE ANOTHER STICK AND WRITE ON IT, "FOR JOSEPH (THE STICK OF EPHRAIM/ SAMARIA) AND ALL THE HOUSE OF ISRAEL ASSOCIATED WITH IT" (this was the Northern Kingdom); AND JOIN THEM TOGETHER INTO ONE STICK, SO THAT THEY MAY BECOME ONE IN YOUR HAND.

EZEK 37:15-17

OUR IMAGE OF A WELL PROBABLY LOOKS LIKE THIS.

ANCIENT WELLS WERE SIMPLY HOLES IN THE GROUND WITH A STONE ACROSS THE TOP. THE TEXT ACTUALLY SAYS THAT JESUS SAT ON THE WELL, SO HE IS PROBABLY SITTING ON THE STONE ABOVE THE MOUTH OF THE WELL.

A FRIENDLY GUIDE TO JOHN'S GOSPEL

Ezekiel acts out this reunification, joining the two sticks, then speaks in God's name saying:

> THUS SAYS THE LORD GOD: I WILL TAKE THE PEOPLE OF ISRAEL FROM THE NATIONS AMONG WHICH THEY HAVE GONE, AND WILL GATHER THEM FROM EVERY QUARTER, AND BRING THEM TO THEIR OWN LAND. I WILL MAKE THEM ONE NATION IN THE LAND, ON THE MOUNTAINS OF ISRAEL; AND ONE KING SHALL BE KING OVER THEM ALL. NEVER AGAIN SHALL THEY BE TWO NATIONS, AND NEVER AGAIN SHALL THEY BE DIVIDED INTO TWO KINGDOMS. THEN THEY SHALL BE MY PEOPLE, AND I WILL BE THEIR GOD.
>
> **EZEK 37:21-23**

When Judah and Samaria are reunited, then God promises to dwell with them.

> I WILL MAKE A COVENANT OF PEACE WITH THEM; IT SHALL BE AN EVERLASTING COVENANT WITH THEM; AND I WILL BLESS THEM AND MULTIPLY THEM, AND WILL SET MY SANCTUARY AMONG THEM FOREVERMORE. MY DWELLING PLACE SHALL BE WITH THEM; AND I WILL BE THEIR GOD, AND THEY SHALL BE MY PEOPLE. THEN THE NATIONS SHALL KNOW THAT I THE LORD SANCTIFY ISRAEL, WHEN MY SANCTUARY IS AMONG THEM FOREVERMORE.
>
> **EZEK 37: 26-28**

THE ENCOUNTER AT JACOB'S WELL

Knowing this background, the scene is set for a meeting between a man from Judea (the Southern Kingdom) and a woman from Samaria (the Northern Kingdom). At first, there is hostility from the woman, but then Jesus speaks of a gift of living water that he can offer. The woman, who thinks he is simply talking about water from the well, challenges him since Jesus has no bucket so how could he draw water from this well. She mockingly asks, "Are you greater than our father Jacob?" (4:12). There were traditions that when Jacob came to the well and met Rachel, a miracle happened: as he lifted the stone the water came rushing up and overflowed for 20 years. Jacob did not need a bucket. This legend lies behind the woman's question to Jesus. Are you greater than Jacob? Can you work a miracle like he did?

Jesus' reply leads the woman deeper as he offers her a gift of 'water' that will well up to eternity-life. Just as natural water gives ordinary human life, Jesus is offering something that will lead to a new quality of life: a share of God's life in eternity. Jesus is definitely greater than Jacob!

The woman now shows a major change of attitude as she asks for this 'water'.

Jesus then sends the woman to get her husband and the woman's response indicates that she has had a total of six husbands: five previously and a current husband. It is most important that we are tuned to the deeper symbolism of this story. Within Judaism, some numbers had special significance. The number seven represented wholeness, completion, perfection. God only needed seven days to complete the work of creation. With seven representing perfection, the number six comes to represent incompleteness, almost but not yet perfect. You might recall that at the wedding in Cana, there were six stone water jars. Here, at Jacob's well, the woman admits to six husbands. Knowing the deeper symbolism of the Gospel, where Jesus is the bridegroom, and the Old Testament background of wells as places of a betrothal, the reader should understand that Jesus is to be the seventh, the Divine bridegroom. Jesus is acting out the prophecy of Ezekiel where God seeks to re-unite Jews and Samaritans into one people and then God's sanctuary will be set among them.

Although this Old Testament imagery of the covenant as a marriage, and God as Israel's bridegroom is unfamiliar to us, it would be very familiar to Jews and Samaritans. The woman is able to follow the deeper symbolic logic of this discussion for she now considers that Jesus may be a prophet and so asks him about proper worship. Jews worshipped on the Temple Mount in Jerusalem, while the Samaritans had built their own Temple on the mountain behind Jacob's well. Jesus' response points to the inadequacy of any building. True worship can only happen in Spirit.

Following this conversation, the woman is the first in the Gospel to recognise Jesus as the Messiah. She leaves the well and through her witness the villagers come and invite Jesus to dwell with them. When Jesus, the Jew, dwells with the Samaritans for some days, the words of Ezekiel are complete:

I will make them one nation in the land, on the mountains of Israel ... My dwelling place shall be with them

Jews and Samaritans are now one, and Jesus, the living Temple, dwells with them.

JOHN 5-10
THE FEASTS OF THE JEWS

Across chapters 5 to 10, the Gospel places Jesus at a series of major Jewish festivals that follow the liturgical cycle: the spring festival of Passover (John 6), the autumn festival of Tabernacles (John 7:1–10:21) and the winter festival of Dedication (Hanukkah). These annual festivals are introduced by the weekly festival of the Sabbath (John 5).

Consider for a moment the members of John's community who have becomes followers of Jesus and have their origins within Judaism. These disciples would have grown up following the cycle of these great festivals within their family. Each year, as they participated in these week-long feasts, they recalled the many ways God had been a saving presence to their ancestors throughout their long history. These festivals were marked with great joy, rich rituals, and often with particular foods. In becoming a disciple of Jesus, does this mean they have lost these feasts and more importantly have they lost touch with the saving presence of God celebrated in these feasts? This is the historical situation of the community that John needs to address with deep theological insight and pastoral sensitivity.

MAJOR JEWISH FESTIVALS

Passover, Pentecost, and Tabernacles were pilgrim feasts when all male Israelites were expected to travel to the Temple in Jerusalem for the week-long festivals. These three feasts look back to the Exodus and the time when they were in the wilderness of Sinai. Dedication is a later festival, celebrating the liberation from Greek domination during the time of the Maccabees (164 BCE).

Other important Holy Days are the Day of Atonement (Yom Kippur), New Year (Rosh Hashanah), and Purim. These are one-day feasts.

THIS IS AN IMAGE OF THE EARTH'S NAVEL, NOW LOCATED IN THE TOMB OF THE RESURRECTION IN JERUSALEM.

DID YOU KNOW?
- Jerusalem was known as the Earth's Navel, connecting heaven and earth (Ezek 38:12).

Note: The Seasons follow the Northern Hemisphere.

Weekly
Sabbath
Creation and liberation from slavery

Spring (April)
Passover (Pesah)
Exodus. The escape from Egypt

Summer (June)
Weeks/Pentecost (Shavuot)
The making of the Covenant at Sinai and gift of the Law

Autumn (September)
Tabernacles/Booths (Sukkot)
God's protection in the Sinai wilderness

Winter (December)
Dedication (Hanukkah)
The Rededication of the Temple in 164 BCE

ARCHAEOLOGICAL REMAINS OF THE ANCIENT HEALING SITE OF BETHESDA.

A MODEL OF THE SHEEP POOLS OF JERUSALEM. IN THE BACKGROUND IS THE ROMAN FORTRESS OF ANTONIA.

DID YOU KNOW?

◆ Archaeologists have discovered an ancient healing pool with five porticos in Jerusalem, very close to the Temple and the Sheep Pool. This is just one of a number of references in John's Gospel that have been verified by archaeology.

JOHN 5
THE SABBATH

At the heart of the controversy that erupts in chapter 5, is the issue of God's ongoing work. The initial verses describe a typical healing miracle, which could be a cause of joy, but then the reader discovers a problem – "Now that day was the Sabbath" (5:9). According to Jewish law, various activities were forbidden on the Sabbath as a way of remembering that God worked for six days but then rested on the seventh: the Sabbath day (Gen 2:2–3).

When the Jerusalem authorities hear about Jesus' healing action, they challenge him (5:16). In response to their hostility Jesus says, "My father is still working, and so am I" (v 17). This leads to a further charge; not only was Jesus breaking the Sabbath he was also blaspheming in calling God his Father "making himself equal to God" (v 18).

Jewish theology recognised that God did not in fact cease all work on the Sabbath day, for on this day children were born and people died. So God obviously continued to 'work' giving life, and judging, since it was their theology that at death a person faced God's judgement. On the Sabbath, Jesus has restored a man to the fullness of life, and has spoken to him a word of judgement in saying, "Sin no more" (v 14). Just as the Father continues to work on the Sabbath, so does Jesus.

When charged with blasphemy in making himself *equal to God*, Jesus provides a small parable that draws upon daily life in Palestine. He uses the example of a son who is an apprentice to his father, and who learns by watching his father and doing what he does (v 19). This parable places the focus of authority on the father-figure, with a son working and learning under the authority of his father. They are not equal.

Jesus then continues by applying the parable to his own situation. It is the Father who raises the dead and pronounces judgement for life with God (eternity-life) or death (spiritual death). The father has given the Son his own authority and so the Son is able to offer eternity-life to those who believe in him.

Here it is important to note that John's Gospel is written from a perspective that the gift of eternity-life is a present reality, it is a gift being given now to those who believe (v 24). In verse 25 we read, "The hour is coming *and now is*, when the dead will hear the voice of the Son of God and those who hear will live." At this point, "the dead" are those who have not yet heard the voice of Jesus and so are spiritually *dead*. Then in verse 28, he speaks of those who are physically dead and buried, those who are "in the tombs". At the voice of the Son, these will come forth to face the consequences of the choices they have made. For those who have led righteous lives, resurrection will be for life. For those who have done evil, their resurrection will be for judgement (v 29).

The legal debate in this chapter is based on Jesus' right to act as the Sabbath God by continuing to work on the Sabbath in giving life and passing judgement. For the Jerusalem authorities, they are not satisfied by Jesus' response and this debate will continue in later chapters. For the Johannine community, they have the affirmation that faith in Jesus does not mean the loss of the Sabbath or the God of the Sabbath. In Jesus, the God of the Sabbath is present in their midst offering life, and through the choices people make to believe in him or not to believe, they are right now coming under judgement.

JOHN 6 THE JEWISH FESTIVAL OF PASSOVER

The greatest saving action of God in Israel's history was the escape from Egypt under the leadership of Moses around the year 1250 BCE. The book of Exodus, describes the series of saving actions: The call of Moses (Exod 3:1–12), the revelation of God's Divine name (Exod 3:13–17), the escape from Egypt's armies (Exod 14), the gift of the manna in the wilderness of Sinai (Exod 16:13–21), the revelation of God to the people at Sinai (Exod 19), the gift of the Law as a pattern of life for God's people to live by (Exod 20), and the making of the great covenant with all the people of Israel (Exod 24).

The Passover festival was commemorated with two powerful symbols: the sacrificial lamb and unleavened bread.

On the eve of the escape, the people sacrificed a lamb, ate the flesh and smeared the blood over their houses so the Angel of God would Passover their homes but smite the Egyptians (Exod 12:1–13). Every year in the Jerusalem Temple, pilgrims would come to sacrifice a lamb for their household, then eat the lamb in a ritualised meal while they told the story of their escape.

The second symbol was that of eating unleavened bread for seven days (Exod 12:14–20). This recalled the haste in which they left Egypt, so there was no time to use leaven/yeast and allow the bread to rise. Over time, the Festival of Unleavened Bread was also linked with the gift of manna, which was called the "Bread from Heaven" (Exod 16:4), or the "food of Angels" (Wis 16:20). A festival of liberation was a time of heightened Jewish expectation that God would deliver them by raising up a new saviour figure such as Moses, or the Messiah.

All the Gospels relate a miracle where Jesus feeds a great multitude with a few loaves of bread and some fish. John's Gospel follows the miracle with a long discourse to bring out the meaning of this miracle, or sign as this Gospel names them. John situates the feeding in the context of the Passover and the seven-day festival of Unleavened Bread. After the miracle, the crowd seek Jesus then ask for a sign that they should believe in him. In the Old Testament, when God called Moses, he was given signs to indicate his authority to the people, so the crowd recall one of these Mosaic signs. "Our Father's ate the manna in the wilderness" (6:31). Jesus responds by pointing out that the gift of bread from heaven was not from Moses but from God. He then speaks of himself as the Father's gift: "My Father gives you the true bread from heaven. For the bread of God is that which comes down from heaven, and gives life to the world" (6:32–33). When the crowd asks for this bread, Jesus replies: "I am the bread of life" (6:35). Jesus is the true gift of God who has come down from heaven to offer not simply nourishment for this life, but nourishment for eternity life. "Everyone who sees the Son and believes in him shall have eternity-life" (6:40). You might recall from the discussion with Nicodemus and

An ancient synagogue in Sephoris, about five kilometres from Nazareth, had this Zodiac with the 12 astrological signs on the floor. At the lower right, you can clearly see the months associated with Winter: Libra (the scales), Scorpio, and Orion the Hunter.

This synagogue is dated to the 5th century CE.

Below are photos of Orion/Sagittarius and Scorpio.

LOAVES AND FISHES MOSAIC FROM THE FLOOR OF A 5TH CENTURY CHURCH ON THE SHORE OF LAKE GALILEE. THE ORIGINAL CHURCH WAS BUILT AROUND 350 CE NEAR THE SITE OF THE FEEDING MIRACLE.

the Samaritan Woman that when this Gospel uses the expression *eternal life*, I choose to translate it *eternity-life* to convey that this is not simply ordinary life going on forever, but is a new quality of life, the very life God lives in eternity. Using the image of bread and nourishment, Jesus speaks of himself as one able to give this quality of life.

Jesus contrasts the nourishment he offers for eternity-life, with the nourishment offered by the manna, which although eaten by their ancestors did not prevent death. "I am the living bread which came down from heaven; whoever eats of this bread, will live into eternity" (6:51).

Up until this point in the discussion, John has drawn upon symbols from within Judaism, such as the nourishment of the manna to speak of Jesus' identity and his instruction. Disciples who turned from Judaism to faith in Jesus could still celebrate Passover and receive the nourishment of the "bread from heaven" in Jesus' teaching. Those disciples who lived during the time of Jesus could express their faith in him by following him. But what about John's community, living some 60 years after the death of Jesus? How could they, and all later Christians, express their faith in Jesus and be nourished by him?

In verse 51, Jesus stops speaking about eating bread and begins to speak of eating "my flesh" and drinking "my blood". This marks a turning point in the discussion. Within Judaism, there are various terms used to speak of the experience of being human under different aspects. Flesh is that aspect of a human being that will corrupt and die. It is a way of speaking of humanity as *mortal*. Blood is associated with life. Within Judaism, blood is drained from meat as the blood represents the life fluid that belongs to God and is forbidden (Gen 9:3–4). To speak of flesh and blood together, is to speak of the whole living human person. When Jesus speaks of eating his flesh and drinking his blood, he is referring to the future when he has passed through death as a mortal being and in his resurrection returned to life. In this passage, John is speaking of the Eucharistic experience of the post-Easter community in whom the living Jesus is encountered and celebrated. Disciples in the future will be able to express their faith in Jesus when they gather for Eucharist. The real presence of Jesus lives on in the community so that disciples of all time continue to experience him and make their faith commitment to him.

Disciples who make the choice for Jesus have not lost the celebration of Passover. The "Bread from heaven", once offered to Israel's ancestors, is now offered to all generations and this *bread* is a gift of nourishment for eternity life.

JOHN 7–8 THE FEAST OF TABERNACLES (SUKKOT – BOOTHS OR SHELTERS)

The Feast of Tabernacles was the most joyful of the feasts. It was a seven-day pilgrim festival celebrated in the autumn. During these days, the pilgrims made booths recalling Israel's time in the wilderness following their escape from Egypt. During this time, they lived in temporary shelters. This festival may have its origins in an ancient harvest festival when farmers stayed out in the fields while harvesting the olives and grapes.

During the time in the wilderness, God cared for the Israelites providing them with manna (Exod 16) and water (Exod 17), and guiding them by the fiery cloud of God's glory (Exod 13:21). At the time of Jesus, the festival was celebrated by three rituals.

 Every morning the priests led a procession from the Temple to the Pool of Siloam to collect a pitcher of water. This water would then be carried back and poured out on the altar. The people would sing psalms and wave a collection of branches of myrtle, palm, and willow trees. While giving thanks for the past gift of water, the people prayed that God would send the autumn rains and looked to a future time when God would send a new saviour like Moses.

 Every evening four huge menorahs (seven-branched candlesticks) were set up in the Temple and the male pilgrims danced under these lights. It was said that these lights lit up every courtyard in Jerusalem.

 A third ritual was carried out every morning by the priests. This ritual recalled a time when the people turned to idolatry and even worshipped the sun (Ezek 8:16). The priests now reversed that act of idolatry and affirmed their faith in Israel's God. The priests went to the East gate of the Temple and stood facing the rising sun, with their back to the Temple. At the moment of sunrise, they turned around to face the Holy of Holies and prayed: "Our fathers when they were in this place turned with their backs toward the Temple of the Lord and their faces toward the east, and they worshipped the sun; but as for us, our eyes are turned to the Lord".

In this festival, these three rituals will be re-interpreted in the light of Jesus.

If you recall, in chapter 5, Jesus had been in conflict with the Jerusalem authorities about his healing of a man on the Sabbath. Now that Jesus is back in Jerusalem this conflict continues. Jesus defends his right to heal a person on the Sabbath because even on the Sabbath a Jewish male child is circumcised (7:21–24). Because the feast is associated with the hope of a future saviour figure, some in the crowd are wondering if Jesus could be the Messiah: "Can it be that the authorities really know that this is the Christ (in Hebrew: Messiah)" (7:26).

On the last day, possibly the added eighth day when the water and light ceremonies had finished, Jesus proclaimed, "If anyone thirst let him come to me and drink. Whoever believes in me, as scripture says, 'Out of his heart will flow rivers of living water'" (7:37–38). There are multiple problems with this verse, including the fact that there are two different versions in the ancient manuscripts that can lead to two different translations. The translation here suggests that living water will flow from the heart of the believer. Another translation reads that the living waters flow from the heart of Jesus. Scholars are almost equally divided on what is meant. Here I will offer my understanding.

The original Pool of Siloam was only discovered recently when workmen were laying a new pipe in Jerusalem. Only part of the pool has been excavated.

Notice the holes at the side of the pool for holding water jars.

DID YOU KNOW?

- In many of the earliest manuscripts, the episode of the woman caught in adultery (John 8:2-11) is not found here in the Gospel of John. Some manuscripts have it in Luke's Gospel (after 21:38 or 24:53). Some have it at the end of John's Gospel.

- The Pool of Siloam was part of the early water system for Jerusalem. A tunnel built in the time of Hezekiah (c. 700 BCE) brought water from outside the city walls to within the city so that the city would have a source of water during a time of siege.

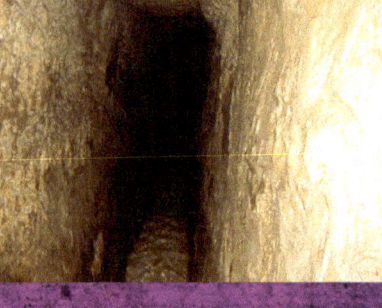

- This picture was taken while walking through Hezekiah's tunnel. Notice the water that still flows from the Gihon spring.

- The text in current bibles was divided into chapters and verses in 1551 by Robert Stephanus. In its original form, there would have been no break between the beginning of the Feast of Tabernacles (7:1) until the mention of the next feast at 10:22. Having chapters and verses can sometimes hinder our reading of the text.

While Jesus is involved in his ministry, he is able to offer living water. You might recall the discussion with the Samaritan woman where Jesus offers her this gift. The symbolism is related to the way this Gospel presents Jesus as the true Temple of God's presence, and the Jewish understanding that the Temple was situated above the source of all the waters of creation. These verses (7:37–38) and the verse that follows – "Now this he said about the Spirit, which those who believed in him were to receive; for as yet the Spirit had not been given, because Jesus was not yet glorified" (7:39) – look ahead to a future time when Jesus is no longer present with the community as he was during his ministry. At that time, it will be the community of believers who will continue to be a living Temple of God in the world, and so the believer, like Jesus, will continue to be a source of living water. I see in this verse a clue that the symbolism of the Temple, which was applied to Jesus in chapter 2, will be transferred to the believers in the future through the gift of the Spirit.

Following this statement about "living waters", Jesus then says, "I am the light of the world; whoever follows me will not walk in the darkness, but will have the light of life" (8:12).

The two great symbols of this festival have now been appropriated by Jesus. Jewish believers in Jesus need not fear that they have lost the Feast of Tabernacles and all that it means. In Jesus, they have the living Tabernacle of God's presence, and in him they have the light of the world and source of living water.

JOHN 9:1-10:22
THE BLIND MAN RESTORED TO SIGHT

The Feast of Tabernacles continues into the episode of the man born blind where the main symbols of the feast are dramatised. In the feast, Jesus had claimed to be a source of living water (7:37–38) and the light of the world (8:12), in John 9 these claims are enacted when Jesus gives sight to a man born in darkness and sends the man to wash in the waters of Siloam. You might recall that the Pool of Siloam was the water source for Jerusalem and every morning during Tabernacles the people would process to the pool to draw water to pour on the altar. In John 9, we are told that the name *Siloam* means sent. Across the Gospel, Jesus is referred to as the one sent from God, so in fact Jesus is the *Sent One*. The man is brought into the light through the power of Jesus. The third ritual of Tabernacles was the morning worship of God when the priests refuted the idolatrous worship of the sun. When the blind man has his sight restored, he professes his faith in Jesus: "Lord, I believe; and he worshipped him" (9:38). His faith is then contrasted with the lack of faith by the Pharisees who through John 9 question the once blind man about how his sight was restored.

When Jesus confronts the Jerusalem leaders, he draws upon an Old Testament image of leadership, that of the good shepherd. This image recalls that David, Israel's great king, was once a shepherd. The prophet Ezekiel, at the time of the Exile in Babylon (587 BCE), criticised the leaders of Judah and called them false shepherds. Because these leaders had not cared for the people,

Ezekiel declares that God will be the true shepherd of Israel. "Thus says the Lord God, 'I myself will be the shepherd of my sheep. I will seek the lost, I will bring back the strayed, I will bind up the crippled and I will strengthen the weak'" (Ezek 34:15–16). In his dispute with the leaders of Jerusalem, Jesus draws on this image to speak of himself: "I am the good shepherd. The good shepherd lays down his life for his sheep" (10:11). Where the one who is hired has no real care and flees when threatened, the Good Shepherd knows his sheep and is prepared to give his life for them.

Throughout the Gospel, some of the people have looked to Jesus as the long-awaited Jewish Messiah, the one expected at the end of time to bring about the reign of God in peace and justice. Frequently the people want a political Messiah like David, a warrior who will liberate them from Rome. Jesus refuses to accept these messianic images. The one image he will accept is that of the messianic good shepherd, prepared to lay down his life.

JOHN 10:22-42
THE FESTIVAL OF DEDICATION (HANUKKAH) (2 MACCABEES 10)

The Jewish Festival of Hanukkah frequently coincides with the Christian festival of Christmas. The Hanukkah lampstand has eight candles rather than the usual seven, to recall the eight days of the festival.

Unlike the festivals of Passover, Tabernacles, and Pentecost, the Festival of Hanukkah was not associated with the Exodus nor was it one of the Pilgrim Festivals. This feast has its origins in the later time when the Jewish people were under the dominion of the Greek Empire. The feast celebrates the great victory by Judas Maccabeus over the Greek ruler Antiochus IV and the rededication of the Temple in 164 BCE. Antiochus had tried to force Greek customs and worship onto the people and gave himself the title *Epiphanes*, or *God Manifest*. He had a pagan altar built in the Jerusalem Temple and ordered sacrifices to be offered to the Greek god Zeus. Led by the Maccabees, the Jewish people drove out the Greeks and established their own independent Jewish kingdom. They then purified the Temple of its defilement and rededicated it to Israel's God. The festival is associated with lights and fire, although the source of this association is not known. There is a legend that when the Jews reclaimed the Temple, they found one jug of unpolluted oil that miraculously kept the lamps alight for eight days.

During this festival, Jesus is again in the Temple, and once again is asked if he is the Messiah. At a festival celebrating Jewish independence, the Jews were no doubt longing for a liberator like David, but Jesus replies in terms of the Messianic image of the shepherd. "My sheep hear my voice, I know them and they follow me; and I give them eternity life" (10:27–28). Within this feast celebrating the re-consecration of the Temple, Jesus speaks of himself as the one "whom the father has consecrated and sent into the world". When his words are rejected, Jesus leaves the Temple for the last time.

* * * * * * *

SHEPHERDS MINDING THEIR SHEEP.

THIS PHOTO SHOWS A LARGE HANUKKAH LAMPSTAND NEXT TO THE WESTERN WALL OF THE TEMPLE MOUNT IN JERUSALEM.

A FRIENDLY GUIDE TO JOHN'S GOSPEL

MENORAH

This is a photo of a floor mosaic from the 5th-century synagogue in Sephoris, showing a typical 7-branched menorah.

DID YOU KNOW?

- The menorah symbolised the presence of God in the burning bush when God's name was revealed to Moses (Exodus chapter 3). It may also represent the tree of life found in Eden (Gen 2:9).

Across these series of feasts, their symbols and meaning have been re-interpreted by John to show that Jesus is now the one in whom all these feasts can find their true meaning. The many blessings of God bestowed on Israel are now brought to their perfection in Jesus.

Around the same time as the Gospel of John was written, a Jewish writer was reflecting on the loss of the Temple and its festivals. The writer of 2 Baruch states:

THE WHOLE PEOPLE ANSWERED AND THEY SAID TO ME:

"FOR THE SHEPHERDS OF ISRAEL HAVE PERISHED, AND THE LAMPS WHICH GAVE LIGHT ARE EXTINGUISHED, AND THE FOUNTAINS FROM WHICH WE USED TO DRINK HAVE WITHHELD THEIR STREAMS. NOW WE HAVE BEEN LEFT IN THE DARKNESS AND IN THE THICK FOREST AND IN THE ARIDNESS OF THE DESERT."

AND I ANSWERED AND SAID TO THEM:

"SHEPHERDS AND LANTERNS AND FOUNTAINS CAME FROM THE LAW AND WHEN WE GO AWAY, THE LAW WILL ABIDE. IF YOU, THEREFORE, LOOK UPON THE LAW AND ARE INTENT UPON WISDOM, THEN THE LAMP WILL NOT BE WANTING AND THE SHEPHERD WILL NOT GIVE WAY AND THE FOUNTAIN WILL NOT DRY UP".

2 BAR 77:11, 13-16

Just as Baruch offers consolation to the Jews who have now lost their Temple and so no longer have the great Temple Festivals, John offers consolation to his community that they have not abandoned the essentials of their Jewish history, religious traditions, and relationship with God. Where the post-70 Jews look to the Law, the Johannine Christians are encouraged to look to Jesus as the light, the source of water, and the shepherd.

JOHN 11-12
THE RAISING OF LAZARUS AND CONSEQUENCES

Chapters 11 and 12 are a transition between the public ministry of Jesus found in the Book of Signs (chapters 1–10) and his final words with the disciples leading into his passion and resurrection found in the Book of Glory (chapters 13–20). The raising of Lazarus is the final dramatic sign of Jesus' authority, confirming what he has said about himself and his relationship with God. At the same time, it is because of Lazarus that crowds from Jerusalem flock to Jesus to such an extent that the authorities are afraid that his popularity could cause trouble with Rome. "What are we to do? For this man performs so many signs. If we let him go on like this, everyone will believe in him, and the Romans will come and destroy, both our holy places and our nation" (11:47–48). This leads to the reply by the high priest, Caiaphas, "it is expedient for you that one man should die for the people, and that the whole nation may not perish" (11:50).

As explained earlier, Jewish belief in life after death was a very late development in Judaism. By the first century, there were two approaches to this issue. The belief of the Pharisees was that there would be a resurrection at the end of time. This would be followed by judgement and then the righteous would live with God. The Book of Wisdom, written around 50 BCE – 50 CE, offers an alternative view. Wisdom teaches that even now, in this life, individuals who choose to live a good life can be given the gift of God's own eternity-life, and this gift continues through death into life forever with God. This view has no need for a future resurrection of the body but does not entirely rule out this possibility. John's Gospel takes up the view of the Book of Wisdom that eternity-life is a present reality.

When Jesus arrives, Lazarus has been in the tomb for four days (11:39). Jewish belief held that the spirit of a person did not truly depart the body until the processes of decomposition began, around four days after death. From this time, the process of death was irreversible. Martha's words to Jesus express conventional belief in the future resurrection. "I know that he will rise again in the resurrection of the last day" (11:24). This is not sufficient Johannine faith.

Jesus responds: "I am the resurrection and the life; whoever believes in me, though he die [like Lazarus], yet shall he live" and he continues, "Whoever lives and believes in me [like the current disciples] shall never die" (11:26). These statements address a real issue not only for Lazarus and his family, but also for the later Johannine Christians. In the first years after Jesus' death and resurrection, the early believers considered that the End Times had arrived and that therefore they would not die. They believed that they were already living with the Spirit and the Risen Jesus, while awaiting his return in glory, which they expected any day. Death had lost its meaning. As time passed and Jesus did not return, and some believers began to die, there was concern about Jesus' promises and what would happen to the dead. Can there be death when Jesus had promised eternity-life?

Jesus' words to Martha affirm that in him there is a quality of life that continues beyond death, for those currently alive and even for those like Lazarus who have already died. The miracle that then happens confirms the truth of his words. Death is not a dead-end.

A TYPICAL ROLLING STONE TOMB

The tomb is a cave with niches in the walls where the body is laid. The mouth of the cave can be closed by a circle-shaped stone rolled back into a groove. Inside this tomb was a ledge on which the body would be laid and prepared for burial by anointing and wrapping in linen clothes. After this, the body would be slid into the wall niches. A light covering would seal these niches and the body left for about a year for decomposition to occur. The stone would be rolled back in place sealing the tomb. If another family member died, they would be interred in another niche in this one tomb.

About a year later, the family would return to the tomb, open the niche, and remove the remains, which by this time would be just bones. The bones would be cleaned and placed in a burial box (*ossuary*) which would be decorated and perhaps the person's name inscribed on it, then this box could be buried, or left in the tomb. This form of burial occurred during the first century until the year 70 CE, while there was political stability.

JOHN 12
THE ANOINTING AND ENTRY TO JERUSALEM

The raising of Lazarus continues to influence events in chapter 12. Jesus remains in Bethany, the home of Martha, Mary, and Lazarus. Bethany is about four kilometres from Jerusalem over Mt Olives. We are told it is six days before the Passover, which is the third Passover of John's Gospel. During a supper, Mary anoints the feet of Jesus with a lavish amount of costly ointment (12:3). Luke also has an episode of a woman washing Jesus' feet (Luke 7:36–50), while Mark (14:3–9) and Matthew (26:6–13) have the unnamed woman anoint

THESE OSSUARIES WERE FOUND ON MT OLIVES.

DID YOU KNOW?

- The very ornate ossuary of Caiaphas, the High priest, was found in 1990 and is now held in the Israel Museum in Jerusalem. It was inscribed 'Joseph, son of Caiaphas'.
- The Tomb of King Herod the Great was only discovered in 2007. He was buried in a specially constructed 'mountain' known as the Herodium, situated on the road to Bethlehem.

Jesus on the head. It is difficult to determine exactly what event lies behind these different narratives. In John, this gesture is an extravagant sign of hospitality towards Jesus, which he will emulate in the next chapter, when he washes the feet of his disciples.

The next day, when Jesus comes from Bethany across Mt Olives into Jerusalem, a great crowd gathers and welcome him as "the King of Israel" (12:13). The action of Jesus riding into Jerusalem on a young donkey recalls the action of Solomon after he was anointed King of Israel.

The response of the Pharisees is to say, "You see that you can do nothing; look the world has gone after him" (12:19). This is immediately followed by the arrival of some Greeks, who are most likely Gentiles, who want to meet Jesus. These Gentiles fulfil the words of the Pharisees that the whole world is now going to Jesus.

The coming of Gentiles to Jesus fulfils the Old Testament prophecies that in the last days the Gentiles (often simply called the 'nations') would also come to Jerusalem to worship Israel's God.

> SO THE PRIEST ZADOK, AND THE PROPHET NATHAN, WENT DOWN AND HAD SOLOMON RIDE ON KING DAVID'S MULE, AND LED HIM TO GIHON. THERE THE PRIEST ZADOK TOOK THE HORN OF OIL FROM THE TENT AND ANOINTED SOLOMON. THEN THEY BLEW THE TRUMPET, AND ALL THE PEOPLE SAID, "LONG LIVE KING SOLOMON!" AND ALL THE PEOPLE WENT UP FOLLOWING HIM, PLAYING ON PIPES AND REJOICING WITH GREAT JOY, SO THAT THE EARTH QUAKED AT THEIR NOISE.
>
> **1 KINGS 1:38-40**

> MANY PEOPLES AND STRONG NATIONS SHALL COME TO SEEK THE LORD OF HOSTS IN JERUSALEM, AND TO ENTREAT THE FAVOR OF THE LORD. THUS SAYS THE LORD OF HOSTS: IN THOSE DAYS, TEN MEN FROM NATIONS OF EVERY LANGUAGE SHALL TAKE HOLD OF A JEW, GRASPING HIS GARMENT AND SAYING, "LET US GO WITH YOU, FOR WE HAVE HEARD THAT GOD IS WITH YOU."
>
> **ZECH 8:22-23**

With the acclamation of the children of Israel and the other nations, represented by the Greeks, Jesus knows that now his public ministry is concluded and his 'hour' can begin.

JESUS SAID, "NOW THE HOUR HAS COME FOR THE SON OF MAN TO BE GLORIFIED. TRULY, TRULY I SAY TO YOU, UNLESS A GRAIN OF WHEAT FALLS INTO THE EARTH AND DIES, IT REMAINS ALONE; BUT IF IT DIES IT BEARS MUCH FRUIT".

JOHN 12:23-24

THE EAST GATE TO JERUSALEM, WHICH FACES THE MOUNT OF OLIVES ON THE EASTERN SIDE OF THE OLD CITY, ALSO KNOWN AS THE GOLDEN GATE AS THIS IS THE GATE THAT THE MESSIAH WILL USE TO ENTER INTO THE CITY AT THE END OF DAYS.

JOHN 13–17 THE FINAL DISCOURSE

Now before the festival of the Passover, Jesus knew that his hour had come to depart from this world and go to the Father. Having loved his own who were in the world, he loved them to the end.

JOHN 13:1-2

These verses provide a solemn introduction to the second part of the Gospel: The Book of Glory. The highpoint of this section, and indeed the entire Gospel, is the Passion narrative, which in this Gospel is called "the hour" and is spoken of as Jesus' exaltation and glorification. "I, when I am lifted up from the earth, will draw all people to myself" (12:32). This is a unique Johannine view of the cross. For John, it is not a scene of degradation or abandonment as in the Synoptics, instead it is the ultimate triumph of Jesus' life and the moment of his return to the Father having accomplished all that he was sent to do.

Prior to the Passion, we read five chapters set in the context of a final meal and in these chapters Jesus offers consolation and reassurance to his disciples; he explains the significance of what is about to happen, teaches the disciples about a future gift of the Spirit and finally prays to the Father. These chapters are similar to a type of writing called a Farewell Testament, which we find in other Jewish writing, when a person offers his final teaching and bequest to his followers as he prepares to die.

There are indications in the text that these five chapters went through stages in their composition. At the end of chapter 14 we read:

"I will no longer talk much with you, for the ruler of this world is coming. He has no power over me; but I do as the Father has commanded me, so that the world may know that I love the Father. Rise, let us be on our way." (14:31–31)

If we then turn immediately to chapter 18, we find:

"After Jesus had spoken these words, he went out with his disciples across the Kidron valley to a place where there was a garden, which he and his disciples entered" (18:1).

It seems there was a time when what we call chapter 18 followed immediately after chapter 14. Scholars consider chapters 13 and 14 were an early form of the discourse and chapters 15, 16, and 17 were written later, by the same author, and added to the Gospel in much the same way that in preparing this book I wrote a first draft, then made changes and developed it further, before sending it to an editor for publishing. In John, these chapters were possibly added to offer further reflections in the light of new historical circumstances facing the community.

When editing ancient manuscripts there was no *cut and paste* as we do today. When adding to a text it would mean inserting a new page.

JOHN 13 THE FOOT WASHING

The 'hour' begins in chapter 13 with the act of Jesus washing the disciples' feet, then interpreting this action firstly as the only way disciples can have any part in him (13:9), then as a model or blueprint for their own behaviour (13:15), and finally as an expression of love (13:34). In that society, foot washing was a common ritual of hospitality and welcome into someone's home, it was also used prior to entering the Temple. Both these meanings need to be considered to understand the meaning of Jesus' act. It is far more than an example of humble service. Through this ritual, Jesus invites and welcomes his disciples to participate in his coming 'hour' and what it will mean for them. In the Synoptic Gospels, on the eve of his death, Jesus used bread and wine to symbolise the meaning of his death as his body given for his disciples. The foot washing has a similar function in John.

When Jesus lays aside and then takes up his garments, these words recall what was said about the Good Shepherd who lays down his life for his sheep and then takes it up again.

'I AM THE GOOD SHEPHERD ... AND I LAY DOWN MY LIFE FOR THE SHEEP. FOR THIS REASON, THE FATHER LOVES ME, BECAUSE I LAY DOWN MY LIFE IN ORDER TO TAKE IT UP AGAIN. NO ONE TAKES IT FROM ME, BUT I LAY IT DOWN OF MY OWN ACCORD. I HAVE POWER TO LAY IT DOWN, AND I HAVE POWER TO TAKE IT UP AGAIN" (10:15, 17–18).

After washing their feet, Jesus says to the disciples, "You do not understand what I am doing now, but you will understand later" (13:7). It is only after the cross that disciples will grasp the deeper symbolism of this action. We will return to this scene later.

JOHN 14 MY FATHER'S HOUSE

Chapter 14 continues to unpack the particular Johannine understanding of Jesus' death. In chapter 14, when Jesus speaks of "my Father's house" and its many dwellings (14:2), we need to recall that he named the Temple, "my Father's house" (2:16).

In the Old Testament, the expression 'my father's house' always refers to the people who make up the household and never to a building; in many modern translations the idiom 'my father's house' is simply translated as 'family' (e.g. Gen 24:38; 28:21;

THE MIDDLE COLUMN OF THIS PAGE FROM *CODEX VATICANUS* IS THE BEGINNING OF THE LETTER TO THE HEBREWS.

'HERE BE DRAGONS!'

A FRIENDLY GUIDE TO JOHN'S GOSPEL

OUR FATHER'S HOUSE

46:31; Josh 2:13). In this introductory phrase (14:2), we need to keep this double meaning in mind – my Father's house – meaning the household and also the Temple.

WARNING!

In the unknown regions of ancient maps they often drew dragons as a warning. Before going any further, I need to offer this warning.

When we read or hear the Gospel in English, very often we miss the meaning of the original Greek words, and sometimes our English translations do not convey the richness of the Greek. This is especially true when reading John 14.

"In my Father's house are many dwellings" (14:2). Often this is incorrectly translated as "many rooms", or "many mansions" this then leads to our imagining heavenly "rooms" where believers will go "up" to after death. This is not what John is saying.

The play on the phrase "my father's house/hold" continues as Jesus speaks of "many dwellings" using a form of the Greek verb *menō* (to dwell). The verb *menō* is then repeated four times in chapter 14 to speak of the Father dwelling in Jesus (14:10); of the Spirit dwelling in believers (14:17); of the Father and Jesus dwelling in the believer (14:23); and Jesus dwelling with the believer (14:25). Translators often use words such as 'abide', or 'live' or 'remain' to translate this one Greek word *menō* and so readers can miss the "many dwellings" Jesus speaks about in this chapter. Jesus speaks of the Father, the Spirit, and himself, dwelling in and with believers. As Jesus prepares to leave his disciples and return to the Father (13:1), he offers them the consolation (see 14:1, 18, 27) of the abiding presence of God; Father, Jesus, and Spirit, in and with the community. Rather than imagining this phrase describing believers going "up" to God, it is expressing God coming "down" to us!

In the Old Testament, the great symbol of God's dwelling in Israel was the Temple, and so chapter 14 is introduced with the phrase Jesus used to speak of the Jerusalem Temple, namely "my father's house" (2:16; 14:2). We see in this chapter a reinterpretation of Israel's Temple traditions to speak of the future Christian community as the dwelling place of God. Somehow, Jesus' departure to the Father, through his death, will bring about the indwelling of God in the community. Believers will be drawn into "my Father's house/hold".

Chapter 14 is like a hologram created through the image of My Father's House which, looked at one way, speaks of the Temple; when looked at another way, speaks of the household, where the household of God consists of the community of believers in whom God dwells, a community which is a living Temple.

RETURNING TO THE FOOT WASHING

Now we can glimpse the deeper symbolism of the foot washing in chapter 13. Jesus washes the feet of his disciples to welcome them into his Father's house: meaning both a household and a Temple. If we were living in the first century, we would be used to this practice of washing one's feet before entering into a home, and before entering into the temple. The foot washing ritual of chapter 13 leads us into the discourse in chapter 14.

One further aspect of chapter 13 needs to be clarified. After the foot-washing, when Jesus has taken up his garments he says, "I have given you a model (*hupodeigma*), that you should do as I have done" (13:15). Once again, the Greek word used here is very important. The word *hupodeigma* is similar to our word *paradigm* and it means a model. It can refer to a model of behaviour, but in the Old Testament it is also used to speak of the 'model' or 'blueprint' for building the tabernacle and the temple, the great symbols of God's dwelling place in Israel (see Exod 25:9; 1 Chron 28:11, 12, 18, 19; Ezek 42:15).

Read in this way, Jesus' act of foot-washing is an act of ultimate love, symbolising his self-giving act of laying down his life. Love is the model or blueprint of the Father's household. Love is the inner dynamism of God and if believers are to be living Temples, members of God's household, then they too must be lovers. Love is the blueprint needed to be part of the Divine Communion of life. Having acted out this love in the foot washing, Jesus then expresses this as his one commandment. "A new commandment I give to you, that you love one another as I have loved you" (13:34).

JOHN 15-17 THE VINE AND THE BRANCHES:

> "DWELL IN ME, AND I IN YOU....I AM THE VINE, YOU ARE THE BRANCHES" (15:4, 5).

Chapter 14 begins with an image of the Temple (the Father's House), then goes on to describe the dwelling of God, Father, Son, Spirit, in the believers, and uses the Greek word *men*, which means to dwell or to abide. This same Greek word continues across chapter 15 but now speaks of the believer dwelling or abiding in Jesus.

It is by abiding, or dwelling in Jesus, that believers are drawn into the heart of the Divine Communion, to dwell or abide in God. Chapters 14 and 15 mirror each other and present a beautiful theology of mutual Divine indwelling: God in us in God. The image of the vine conveys the deep intimacy of this communion as there is no distinguishing the vine from its branches; the vine is the branches.

Chapter 15 also continues the themes of chapter 13 where there was the foot washing, which symbolically demonstrated Jesus' laying down his life, followed by Jesus explaining his action as a model and giving his disciples a new commandment. These themes are now repeated in chapter 15. "This is my commandment, that you love one another as I have loved you. No one has greater love than this, to lay down one's life for one's friends" (15:12–13).

THE PARACLETE

In chapter 14, on the eve of his departure, Jesus consoled his disciples with this promise:

> "AND I WILL ASK THE FATHER, AND HE WILL GIVE YOU ANOTHER PARACLETE*, TO BE WITH YOU FOREVER. THIS IS THE SPIRIT OF TRUTH, WHOM THE WORLD CANNOT RECEIVE, BECAUSE IT NEITHER SEES HIM NOR KNOWS HIM. YOU KNOW HIM, BECAUSE HE DWELLS WITH YOU, AND HE WILL BE IN YOU" (14:16–17).

As we continue to read across these chapters, we hear more about this Paraclete. In the context of the world's hatred and persecution, it is the Paraclete who will enable the disciples to bear witness to Jesus.

> 'IF THE WORLD HATES YOU, BE AWARE THAT IT HATED ME BEFORE IT HATED YOU. ... IF THEY PERSECUTED ME, THEY WILL PERSECUTE YOU. ... WHEN THE ADVOCATE COMES, WHOM I WILL SEND TO YOU FROM THE FATHER, THE SPIRIT OF TRUTH WHO COMES FROM THE FATHER, HE WILL TESTIFY ON MY BEHALF. YOU ALSO ARE TO TESTIFY BECAUSE YOU HAVE BEEN WITH ME FROM THE BEGINNING" (15:18, 20, 26–27).

*Sometimes translated Advocate or Counsellor.

In the future absence of Jesus, it is the Paraclete who will be the ongoing revelation of God to the disciples. The Spirit will be the one to guide the disciples to understand the meaning of Jesus' life, his words and his death and resurrection.

> "I DID NOT SAY THESE THINGS TO YOU FROM THE BEGINNING, BECAUSE I WAS WITH YOU. BUT NOW I AM GOING TO HIM WHO SENT ME; YET NONE OF YOU ASKS ME, 'WHERE ARE YOU GOING?' BUT BECAUSE I HAVE SAID THESE THINGS TO YOU, SORROW HAS FILLED YOUR HEARTS. NEVERTHELESS, I TELL YOU THE TRUTH: IT IS TO YOUR ADVANTAGE THAT I GO AWAY, FOR IF I DO NOT GO AWAY, THE ADVOCATE WILL NOT COME TO YOU; ... I STILL HAVE MANY THINGS TO SAY TO YOU, BUT YOU CANNOT BEAR THEM NOW. WHEN THE SPIRIT OF TRUTH COMES, HE WILL GUIDE YOU INTO ALL THE TRUTH; FOR HE WILL NOT SPEAK ON HIS OWN, BUT WILL SPEAK WHATEVER HE HEARS, AND HE WILL DECLARE TO YOU THE THINGS THAT ARE TO COME." (16:4–7, 12–15).

JESUS' PRAYER

John 17 brings the Final Discourse to a conclusion with an intimate "overhearing" of Jesus as he prays to his father.

Jesus begins by asking that he may return to the glory of his relationship with the Father, having now completed the task given to him: to make God known (17:1–8). He then prays for the disciples, who are to remain in the world, that they will be held or protected in God's name and be made holy in truth (17:9–19). Finally, Jesus prays for the future believers that they too may be drawn into the Divine Communion of life and love shared by Jesus and the Father (17:20–26).

With the abiding presence and guidance of the Paraclete, and held in the prayer of Jesus, believers will not be left as orphans when Jesus returns to the Father. All is now ready for the *hour* to begin.

JOHN 18-19
THE HOUR

At this point, before we begin our reading of the Johannine passion, I want to recall a number of clues that have been given in the preceding chapters. It would be helpful for you to look up these verses, which provide key information about Jesus and the theology of this Gospel.

- The Gospel beings with the opening verse of the Genesis creation account; creation is to be an important theme (1:1).

- The plot of this Gospel is for believers to be born again as children of God (1:11–12; 3:3).

- Jesus is described in terms of Israel's Tabernacle and Temple; he is now the place where God dwells, (1:14; 2:19–21) and in the future believers will also be Temples (7:37–39).

- There is going to be a time, called *the hour*, when the relationship between Jesus and his mother is going to be important (2:3–4).

- The phrase "my Father's house" has a double meaning: both a Temple and a household (2:16; 14:2).

In *the hour*, we will see how all these clues come together in the unique vision of a great artist and theologian.

In order to understand John's particular insight into the meaning of the cross, it is helpful to take notice of some of the unique features found in this Gospel.

Here, I signal three:

1. the creation symbolism
2. the meaning of the title on the cross (19:19)
3. and the significance of the presence of Jesus' mother and the Beloved Disciple at the foot of the cross (19:25–27).

CREATION

The Johannine passion makes use of a number of allusions to the Genesis creation account (Gen 2–3). Only in John's Gospel is Jesus arrested and buried in a garden.

> AFTER JESUS HAD SPOKEN THESE WORDS, HE WENT OUT WITH HIS DISCIPLES ACROSS THE KIDRON VALLEY TO A PLACE WHERE THERE WAS A GARDEN, WHICH HE AND HIS DISCIPLES ENTERED (18:1).
>
> NOW THERE WAS A GARDEN IN THE PLACE WHERE HE WAS CRUCIFIED, AND IN THE GARDEN THERE WAS A NEW TOMB IN WHICH NO ONE HAD EVER BEEN LAID (19:41).

John emphasises that the cross is placed in the middle: "There they crucified him, and with him two others, one on either side, with Jesus in the middle" (19:18). This is similar to the tree of life in the Genesis garden: "The tree of life was also in the middle of the garden" (Gen 2:9).

At the foot of the cross stand a man and a woman, who is only named "woman" and "mother" (19:25–26). These were the names given to Eve. "She shall be called Woman, because she was taken out of Man" (Gen 2:23); "The man called his wife's name, Eve, because she was the mother of all living" (Gen 3:20).

Through these allusions to the Genesis creation stories, it is as if John was painting a picture of the Garden of Eden as the backdrop for his crucifixion account.

While the Synoptics portray the crucifixion drawing on Jewish atonement day symbolism (e.g. the tearing of the Temple veil, Mark 15:38), John presents the cross as an act of creation.

JESUS THE NAZARENE

In this Gospel, the sign above Jesus' head is called a "title" (Gk: *titlon*, 19:19) and it is different from the sign in the Synoptic Gospels where it is called an "inscription" (Mark 15:25; Luke 23:38) and a "charge" (Matt 27:37). Only John's Gospel has the words, "Jesus *the* Nazarene King of the Jews". The phrase, 'Jesus the Nazarene' occurs three times in the Passion, twice in the garden when Jesus is arrested (18: 5, 7), and as the title on the cross (19:19). First-century Jews would understand the scriptural allusions behind the use of this title, "the Nazarene". Firstly, it alludes to the words of Isaiah, "a shoot shall spring from the stock of Jesse, and a branch (Hb: *netzer*) shall grow out of his roots" (Isa 11:1). The word 'branch' in Hebrew is formed from the same consonants (*nzr*) as the word Nazarene. For a first-century Jew, it is as if Jesus dies under the title, 'the Branch'. Secondly, this is the

symbolic title used by the prophet Zechariah to name the one who will build the new Temple in the final age. Zechariah states "*behold the man, whose name is the Branch; ... and he shall build the Temple of the Lord*" (Zech 6:12). This verse from Zechariah is also hinted at in the words Pilate uses to announce Jesus to the crowd, "*Behold the man*" (19:5). Using these prophetic texts from Isaiah and Zechariah, which first-century Jews would readily know, the Johannine title could be rephrased: Jesus the Branch, the Temple builder.

Remember Jesus' words to the Jews in John 2, "Destroy this temple and in three days I will raise it up" (2:19). On the cross, one temple is destroyed – the temple of his body – but the title on the cross suggests that Jesus will also build a temple. Recall also that in the narrative,

A FRIENDLY GUIDE TO JOHN'S GOSPEL

THE RUBELEV ICON OF THE TRINITY, THE HOUSEHOLD OF GOD, DRAWS THE VIEWER INTO THE SCENE, TO TAKE HIS/HER PLACE AT THE TABLE, TO FILL THE EMPTY SPACE AND COMPLETE THE CIRCLE.

the Temple was first named "my Father's house" (and this expression also means the household).

BUILDING THE FATHER'S HOUSE/HOLD

In John's Gospel, Jesus speaks to his mother from the cross saying, "Woman, behold your son" (19:26). He then says to the Beloved Disciple, "Behold your mother" (19:27). These words establish a new relationship between the Beloved Disciple and the mother of Jesus. They are now mother and son. In changing their relationship, Jesus has also changed the relationship of the disciple to himself. If they are now both sons of the one mother, then the Beloved Disciple is now a brother of Jesus. And if the disciple is now a brother of Jesus, it follows that the disciple is also drawn into Jesus' relationship as Son of the Father. To use inclusive language, this scene portrays the Divine filiation of all disciples. In the death of Jesus, disciples become *brothers and sisters* of Jesus and children of God. Disciples are now drawn into the Father's house/hold. Jesus confirms this in his first appearance to Mary Magdalene. "Go to my brothers and sisters and say to them, I am ascending to my Father and *your father*" (20:17).

On the cross, the Temple of his body is destroyed; from the cross, Jesus raises up a new Temple, (the Father's house/hold) in the community of disciples.

Following this change of relationship, the reader is told, "the disciple took her 'to his own'" (*eis ta idia*) (19:27). This phrase was used in the Prologue: "He came to his own (*eis ta idia*) and his own did not receive him; but to all who did receive him, who believed in his name, he gave them the power to become the *children of God*" (1:11–12). Here at the cross, these words of the Prologue are realised, as the Beloved Disciple, representative of all disciples, becomes brother to Jesus and child of God. The disciple is now drawn into the Father's house/hold. In this way, Jesus raises up a new Temple in the Hour: the Temple of his Father's house/hold.

When the side of Jesus is pierced by a lance, we are told that immediately "there came out blood and water" (19:34). This suggests an image of birth. As Jesus said to Nicodemus, "unless one is born again he cannot see the Kingdom of God" (3:3), and also, "unless one is born of water and the spirit, he cannot enter the kingdom of God" (3:5). From the cross, Jesus breathes down the Spirit onto the small group of disciples gathered at the foot of the cross (19:30) and from his side the blood and waters of new birth flow. In this hour, disciples are born anew into the Divine household.

Jesus' final word, "It is finished" (19:30) echoes God's concluding word at the end of creation: "Thus the heavens and earth were finished ... and on the seventh day God finished the work, and rested on the seventh day" (Gen 2:1–2). In John's theology, God continued to work (recall John 5:17: "My Father is still working, and so am I") and creation was only brought to completion at the cross, and John states twice that Jesus' death was followed by the Sabbath (19:31).

Joseph of Arimathea and Nicodemus request that Jesus' body be buried and they prepare his body for burial by anointing it with a lavish amount of spices and fragrant oils fit for a king. He is then buried in a new tomb, and John states that this was in a garden (19:41).

JOHN 20
THE RESURRECTION

In one sense John's Gospel does not need a resurrection since everything has happened at the cross: Jesus has completed his mission and returned to the Father, disciples are now children of God and thus part of the Father's household and a new living Temple where the Father, Son and Spirit dwell. While Jesus' mission has been accomplished, the disciples are yet to realise the meaning of the cross for themselves, and for the world. John 20 is not so much about the resurrection of Jesus but the raising to life of the disciples.

In John 20, there are three scenes and two timeframes. On the first day of the week, the first scene is focused on the empty tomb and what it could mean (20:1–18). Then, in the evening of that same day, the next scene occurs inside a house (20:19–25). Eight days later, the disciples, now with Thomas present, are gathered again inside a house (20:26–29).

Creation symbolism continues as the tomb was in a garden and Mary Magdalene thinks Jesus is the gardener (20:15). (The original gardener in Genesis was God, so Mary Magdalene is ironically correct!) The days that are mentioned, the "first day" and "eight days later", are associated with the dawn of a new creation. The old creation was completed on the seventh day; the eighth day is the first day of a new creation. You might notice that many baptismal fonts and baptisteries have eight sides to signify that in baptism we are reborn into a new creation.

The Temple symbolism is also subtly suggested by the position of the two angels in the tomb. When Mary looks in, she sees the two angels "sitting where the body of Jesus had lain, one at the head, and one at the feet" (20:12). This is the position of the two angels who rested above the Ark of the Covenant within the Holy of Holies.

Mary is the first to receive an appearance of the Risen Jesus and to hear the Easter message: "Go to my brothers and sisters and say to them, I am ascending to my Father and your Father, to my God and your God" (20:17). That evening, the disciples also see the Risen Jesus in their midst. It is only now that disciples are sent on mission. With the gift of the Spirit breathed onto them, they are sent to continue the mission of Jesus in the world. "As the Father has sent me, so I send you. ... Receive the Holy Spirit." (20:21, 22). There are two aspects of this mission. They are sent to forgive sin (20:23), and to gather people: "whoever you hold, are held" (20:23). This phrase (20:23) is often read in the light of the Synoptic expression that speaks of binding and loosing, in relation to Peter's authority (Matt 16:19). While the first part of the phrase clearly states, "if you forgive the sins of any, they are forgiven", the second part does not mention the word sin and is better understood to mean holding firm to one another in community. In Jesus' prayer on the eve of his *hour*, he had prayed, "While I was with them I kept them in you name…; I have guarded them and none of

TOP: THE TOMB OF THE RESURRECTION WITHIN THE BASILICA ORIGINALLY BUILT BY CONSTANTINE IN THE FOURTH CENTURY.

TUCKED AWAY BEHIND THE PILLARS OF THE BASILICA CAN STILL BE SEEN THE REMAINS OF OTHER FIRST-CENTURY TOMBS THAT WERE NOT OBJECTS OF DEVOTION.

THIS PHOTO COMES FROM A MEMORIAL FOR ALL THE JEWS MURDERED IN THE CONCENTRATION CAMP AT SACHSENHAUSEN, ABOUT 30 KILOMETRES FROM BERLIN.

UNLIKE JESUS, MANY OF THESE JEWS HAD NO BURIAL PLACE, FOR THEY WERE BURNED IN THE OVENS.

> When speaking about the Christian "Sabbath", an ancient writer wrote: "NOT THE SABBATHS OF THE PRESENT ERA ... BUT THAT WHICH I HAVE APPOINTED TO MARK THE END OF THE WORLD AND TO USHER IN THE EIGHTH DAY, THAT IS, THE DAWN OF ANOTHER WORLD. THIS, BY THE WAY, IS WHY WE JOYFULLY CELEBRATE THE EIGHTH DAY – THE SAME DAY ON WHICH JESUS ROSE FROM THE DEAD" (Ep. Barn. 15:8-9), Epistle of Barnabus (c. 95-135 CE).

them is lost" (17:12). Now the task of *keeping* and *guarding* is passed onto his disciples.

Eight days later, Jesus appears again, and this time Thomas is present. Thomas had said he would not believe unless he had physical proof. Now, Jesus offers that proof, and Thomas confesses, "My Lord and my God" (20:28). At this point, Jesus turns from his disciples present in the room to gaze into the future, to the disciples *of all time*. Jesus then speaks his blessing on those future disciples, who believe without the privileged seeing of the first community.

> "BLESSED ARE THOSE WHO HAVE NOT SEEN AND YET BELIEVE" (20:29).

This blessing extended towards future believers brings the Gospel to a close. The evangelist finishes with a statement explaining his reason for writing the things that he has and for the choices he has made about what to include in his Gospel: "These things are written that you may believe that Jesus is the Christ, the Son of God, and that believing you may have life in his name" (20:31).

JOHN 21

As stated earlier, chapter 21 is considered by many scholars to be the work of another hand, written probably soon after the death of the Beloved Disciple (21:20–23). This chapter resolves some outstanding issues that had not been dealt with in the preceding narrative. In this chapter, Peter clearly stands out as the leader among the disciples. He initiates the fishing expedition and then is the first to react to the Beloved Disciple's statement of recognition: "It is the Lord" (21:7). During the time of Jesus trial, Peter had denied Jesus three times (18:17, 25, 27), now, on the shores of the Sea of Tiberias, he gives a triple affirmation of his love for Jesus and Jesus confers on him pastoral leadership: "Feed my lambs" (21:15).

It is likely that the Johannine community was led by the disciple known in the text as "the Beloved Disciple". His witness and insight shaped the theological thinking of this group, and with his death the community may have felt doubly bereft. It seems some even thought that he would not die but would be alive for the return of Jesus. At the end of chapter 21, this issue is resolved when Jesus clarifies that he had not said to this disciple that he would not die (21:23).

EARLY MORNING ON THE SHORES OF THE SEA OF TIBERIAS.

OPPOSITE ABOVE: EIGHT-SIDED BAPTISMAL FONT FROM BETHLEHEM.

OPPOSITE BELOW: STATUE OF JESUS AND PETER ON THE SHORES OF THE SEA OF TIBERIAS.

READING JOHN TODAY

> **DID YOU KNOW?**
> - The word ecology comes from the Greek word *oikos*, which means 'house'.

John's Gospel resounds with an affirmation of life. "I have come that you may have life to the full" (10:10). In our own age, this is a message that can speak to the heart of human desires today. Where the Synoptic Gospels work from a theological framework of sin and atonement, John speaks of life and eternity-life. This is an alternative approach to the meaning of Jesus' life, death and rising. The Johannine story of salvation is in essence a love story. God so loved the world, and in love sent Jesus to gather children into the Divine Communion. From John's perspective, creation has been continually unfolding, as life is drawn into a new depth of God's own life, eternity-life. The cross ushers in this new possibility where men and women can know themselves to be children in God's household.

In a world that is becoming more alert to the fragile ecology of our planet, and our small place in a vast cosmological process, a spirituality of dwelling in God's oikos (household) offers a rich biblical and thoroughly Christian dimension to the human desire to live in harmony with God and all creation.

For further details see:

Mary L. Coloe, God Dwells with Us: Temple Symbolism in the Fourth Gospel. Collegeville, MN.: Liturgical Press, 2001.

Mary L. Coloe, Dwelling in the Household of God: Johannine Ecclesiology and Spirituality. Collegeville: Liturgical Press, 2007.

You can also see a lecture by Dr Coloe on the Gospel of John on Youtube.

GOD SO LOVED THE WORLD THAT GOD GAVE THE ONLY SON, THAT WHOEVER BELIEVES IN HIM SHOULD NOT PERISH BUT HAVE ETERNITY-LIFE (3:16).

www.ingramcontent.com/pod-product-compliance
Lightning Source LLC
Chambersburg PA
CBHW061100170426
43199CB00025B/2947